Coming Home

To Lemuria

By Charmian Redwood

OZARK
MOUNTAIN
PUBLISHING

For permission, serialization, condensation, adaptions, or for our catalog of other publications, write to Ozark Mountain Publishing, Inc., P.O. Box 754, Huntsville, AR 72740, ATTN: Permissions Department.

Library of Congress Cataloging-in-Publication Data

Redwood, Charmian, 1951-

Coming Home to Lemuria, by Charmian Redwood

A firsthand account through the use of hypnosis and past life regression of life in Lemuria. The lives we have forgotten as Lemurians. We co-created through instant manifestation with our minds. We are back now to bring these energies through to help our Mother Earth.

1. Lemuria 2. Hypnosis 3. Past-life Regression 4. Metaphysics 5. Co-Creation

I. Redwood, Charmian, 1951- II. Lemuria III. Metaphysics IV. Hypnosis V. Title

Library of Congress Catalog Card Number: 2013933896

ISBN: 9781886940413

Cover Art and Layout: www.noir33.com
Book set in: Times New Roman, Borealis
Book Design: Tab Pillar

Published by:

PO Box 754
Huntsville, AR 72740

WWW.OZARKMT.COM

Printed in the United States of America

ACKNOWLEDGEMENTS

For their continuous love and support of my strange ways, I thank my children Jenny and Tim whose birth started me on this journey home.

Many thanks to George for his generosity and support while I compiled this book.

Then, too, I must thank those who graciously allowed me to lead them into hypnosis to retrieve the information contained here: George Morgan, Aaman Degarth, Elizabeth Keller, Reagan Breen, Kaye Russell, Bahli Mans Morris, Elisha and Jane Stevenson.

Also, I am so grateful to Heather Golding for the beautiful artwork for the cover. The figure in the center represents the heart and creativity of Lemuria while the glyphs surrounding it are creation codes from the Source. www. huulanaya.com

Dear Mother Maui, I thank you for calling me home!

TABLE OF CONTENTS

FOREWORD

HOMECOMING

It is March 2006, and I am flying to Hawaii for the first time—a place I had been dreaming of and longing to visit for twenty years. Half way across the Pacific, I burst into tears because I knew I was coming home. I didn't know what I was coming home to; I just knew that for the first time in my life, I would be "home."

Stepping off the plane onto this sacred land, I was enfolded by the soft, nurturing energy of the Hawaiian islands and knew that here was a place where it was safe to be "me"—one where I could allow myself to show "Who I Am." Part of me had always wanted to remain hidden because it didn't feel safe.

On the second day of my trip, I entered the water at Honaunau and met my dolphin family for the first time. Not only was I home, but here was my family waiting for me.

They said to me, "You need to move here."

I said, "Fine, but I will need a miracle."

I had very little money, no house to sell, and no savings.

That same evening I went to a shamanic drumming circle where the dolphins took me to Sirius to show me where we came from. (That journey is now on a meditation CD on my website.) I mentioned to the group that the dolphins were telling me to live there, and then I was offered six months' house-sitting by an angel in human clothing.

So began my Homecoming.

I returned to Santa Fe, sold everything, and moved to Hawaii on 6/6/06.

Once I settled into life in Hawaii, I began my hypnotherapy work, which I called "Hypnotherapy for the Soul" because it involved connecting clients with their God-selves and spiritual lineage. In all of the clients' journeys, memories of Lemuria came flooding back.

As their stories began to unfold, it became very clear that they were returning Lemurians, and it was time for them to Remember Who They Were/Are. It is their stories that I'm inviting you to hear. Sit back and enjoy. Who knows? These may be your stories, too. First, I'll begin with a brief overview of these individuals' discoveries, remembrances, and memories of Lemuria.

A Brief Overview of Ancient Lemuria

As ancient Lemurians, we came to Earth from various star systems to bring the Pure Light of Love. We chose to come to a predominantly water-covered Earth because our bodies were more subtle than physical, and it was easier for us to enter into a watery environment than to be on land. Thus, we began our Earth adventure in the beautiful oceans of Mother Earth where our subtle bodies could more easily remain connected to Source. We lived in Wholeness and Love, always connected to the Golden Light of the Source.

With our subtle bodies, we propelled ourselves by focusing with intention. We didn't walk with a heavy tread; we connected with the surface in a soft, floating way. Presently, when we walk, we step heavily on the earth and connect with every step. Then it was more like gliding along the ground in a continuous fluid movement as if we were becoming part of the surface.

The whole Lemurian civilization evolved from a small group of Beings using their minds to create everything they needed in a constant flowing movement of forms, which morphed continuously from one form to another. Form evolved from the dust of Earth and the starlight of space. They manifested from nothingness in an ever evolving process as they came into this particular time and space—a temporal moment, a moment in time.

This is who we were as Lemurians—Love, Beauty, and Grace. We stood in the essence of our Being and Love as we walked and worked together. The Light was in everything we did. It was as natural to us as breathing. We breathed Love. We breathed it together. We came into our circles and breathed Love and Light into form. We created beauty with our every breath. We were all connected to Source by a golden thread and lived in harmony and peace with all beings and all kingdoms in constant telepathic communication with all life forms.

Everything that we did in Lemuria before The Fall was for the benefit of the whole. [The Fall was a soul choice we made to disconnect from the Source and live on our own in density. It was a descent into an ego experience so our souls could evolve by overcoming challenges. It involved living in dense bodies—a totally new experience for us. It was a gradual process where our bodies became increasingly dense, and we forgot who we were. Chapter 17 tells this story.] Before this happened, we cared for and included everyone equally. Our sole desire was to serve and assist others to fulfill their service and desires. There was no thought of competition, lack, or scarcity. We created everything that we needed, and there was always enough for everyone.

In Lemuria, we used seed crystals to co-create our world. With a small crystal we were able to tap into a portal where the dimensions melted, and physical laws were bent and changed. We were able to grow a crystal to any size. We even grew merkabas, divine light vehicles used by ascended masters to connect with and reach those in tune with the higher realms. "Mer" means Light. "Ka" means Spirit. "Ba" means Body. Mer-Ka-Ba means the spirit/body surrounded by counter-rotating fields of light, (wheels within wheels), spirals of energy as in DNA, which transport the spirit /body from one dimension to another. The power therein is infinite and contains all the consciousness of the universe.

Source energy coming from crystals generated power to manifest the physical, but it didn't work like what we have in the twenty-first century. It was completely silent and yet very powerful. We used the crystals to amplify our own spirit, intention, and what we wanted to create—anything, even a building or a city. These crystals were able to gather far scattered energies into a cohesive unit, ray, or beam. There were giant generator crystals as big as a building. Some were in geometric shapes while others were domes, which covered buildings.

Everyone was reminded constantly of how much they were loved. The whole society was based on the premise of Love. People were focused on doing everything for the Highest Good of All. Their individual purpose and the collective purpose was Love.

In Lemuria each person had a job and a focus. Society was much like on Earth today with specialized areas of activity, but everyone worked for the good of the whole. There was a network of understanding—almost like a grid of technology— underlying the cities as an invisible grid with lines of light connecting each place to the whole. It was used as a form of communication between places much like we use telephones/cellphones/iphones; however, what was running through the lines was Love. All were communicating telepathically with everyone else about their purpose or focus by using the network of lines of Light like lasers, which ran through the whole city. The lines carried communication about Truth, Light, Love, and how all could support one another and help one another with their tasks. It was truly a feeling of one family, one community, and one Love.

Resurfacing Lemurian Memories

Life in Lemuria was a marriage of God and man, the physical awareness of the body, the self, and the Bliss/Oneness of Beingness with no separation between God consciousness and self. That is not true today on Earth. We need a new language now to speak about this place of selflessness and can only talk about it now in bits and pieces. It's like nothing people can imagine today.

The memories of Lemuria are resurfacing now because as a society we have moved so far away from what really matters. We need to be reminded of our Oneness—all are connected and each has an intricate role to play and a unique gift to share. We can all work in harmony with each one adding to the whole. When we can create Love, we can live Love, peace, and wholeness. We can be creators using conscious creation with male/female energies to return to the Oneness, to the focus of Love, giving our gifts and living our souls' purposes. It's about helping each other and caring for each other selflessly for the good of the greater whole. It's all about connection— remembering who we are—Love!

Some of the individuals telling their Lemurian stories noted that as they look at their lives now, they can see they have always lived life the Lemurian way. As children, they would watch the news of war or see people being hurtful to one another and wonder where they had come to live and who these people were who were hurting each other. Some had always been able to see what people needed and gave it to them if they could or helped others make it happen just because their need was there. Some always wanted to bring people together in community to share projects as well as to share joy and Love. They treated all children as if they were theirs, all elders like their parents, and everyone else like their brother or sister, especially animals, plants, and birds—All One family, All One Love, a Circle of Love, always loving and supporting one another. Their friends are the same way. People tell them they should take care of themselves instead of taking care of everyone else, but when they take care of others, are they not taking care of themselves since all are one?

CHAPTER 1
LEMURIAN CONSCIOUS

A Circular/Spherical Sense of Oneness

Life in Lemuria was a marriage of God and man, the physical awareness of the body, the self, and the Bliss/Oneness of Beingness with no separation between God consciousness and self. In order to speak from this place of selflessness, we would need a new language for we can only talk about it now in bits and pieces. It's like nothing people can imagine today.

Everything we did in Lemuria was circular. Our subtle light bodies were globes of light, and we worked in circles within circles. We could extend our energies so that we were always connected to the others in our circle. We were huge beings, so we could be physically very distant but feel we were close together. We merged with each other in our subtle bodies. Each circle emerged from our core and connected with the others in our team. Also, everything around us vibrated with color and sound. We held the consciousness: I am one with everything. I know everything, and I can manifest anything.

The Universal Eye Unites with the Heart Chakra

In our teams we connected through our third eyes and brought the energy into our hearts. We had a saying, "I see the Eye and the Eye sees me." The Eye put into our consciousness the vast knowing that we could do everything, and we were everything. Nothing was ever in doubt or question; everything was a "yes."

_hat was the purpose of the Eye—to connect with the purpose of Oneness and focus our mutual goal. We worked in our circles because of the Eye, and at the same time the Eye was here because we were anchoring it—each one of us individually and all of us together. We had conscious Oneness with the Eye and could distribute our abilities to any parts of our bodies. We stretched our arms and felt connected to the whole circle. When we brought in our arms, then we used our eyes to see where the others were. We connected to the Universal Eye through our third eye, our higher eye, and in the center of the circle was a connecting eye. We reached out to each other and used that connection to manifest everything we wanted to create.

We connected in the heart with an intention we shared with the collective eye. In this way we shared it with each other. It spread and established very quickly, so we knew that everyone had the same intention. We saw the intention with the third eye, brought it into our hearts and from there, we spread it through our arms, connecting with each other. We used sound to assist in the process of manifesting the intention. We condensed our breathing, breathing sound through the mouths and also tuning in to the appropriate color for what we were manifesting.

We visualized what we wanted to create, and then we breathed into that image. We held the image in the center of the circle at the level of the third eye. The more we breathed sound from our throats, the more the image gained tangible density, form, and shape. We used lines of energy to form patterns, which created the basic structure or matrix around which we wove the form and shape.

Focused Intent

We never had to think about "how" to do anything. We just did it from our hearts, focused with intent and joy—so much joy and bliss. We were constantly moving and vibrating. In the early days of Lemuria, we were particles of light and energy, constantly moving and exchanging information with each other. We would hold our focused intent on the vision. When we held the vision, it was comforting to know that we didn't hold it by ourselves. There was always a circle of other beings of Light.

Other beings were available who knew how to anchor energy with focused intent. We stood in our circle with others and held the image of what we wanted to create in the center of the circle. When it was easy and anchored, we knew it was the right intent because the right use was supported by every part of ourselves. What on present day Earth is now called ego, personality, or all the different fragments that have names were working together in alignment with the Whole. Not one of them was left out or denied because each aspect of our Being contributed its own color or frequency to assist with the focused intent. Before we wanted to create anything, it was very important to recreate a sense of Oneness.

Everybody in Lemuria was in a place of absolute trust and could work together seamlessly. Even though we were in separate bodies, we had a complete connection to Spirit and God and everything around us. Everyone was completely connected in an amazing awareness that God or the Divine was in every being. We radiated that awareness. It was like a geode with little crystals—each a crystal separate and yet part of the whole. It was so peaceful and yet a dynamic whirling of energy and creativity. There was so much Light.

From the Crown Chakra to the Sacral Chakra

In time we knew that it was time to bring the energies and frequencies past the crown, third eye, and heart. Thus, we joined together in our creation circles and wove together the energy of our crown chakras with the continuity of life a major focus of our creations. We had learned to create by focusing on the third eye and heart chakras: it was time to go further and connect to the lower chakras in the energy system—initially with our second chakras where we brought in and held the highest vibrating energy—that of creation. Thus, in order to form a harmonious creation, each member of the circle needed to be aligned in the crown, heart, and sacral chakras. Then the creation was aligned.

Whatever we wanted to create together had to have a masculine and feminine aspect in order to uphold the balance of life. As we function now in a fully activated physical body, everything we create also has a body, but then in our light bodies where everything was one, it was different. We needed to acknowledge the mental and physical aspects and their vital connection to the overall purpose.

The Biggest Challenge—the Root Chakra

Then came our biggest challenge—to bring that high vibration into the root chakra. That was a long process of evolution. It took eons for us to develop that ability. We felt so much more at ease when we just connected in our hearts, and we were in bliss when we connected through the Eye and with the extensions of ourselves. It required conscious, difficult "densification" to bring the energy all the way down to the root chakra.

The sound changed when it went down below the heart. It felt grating, and we had to become comfortable with that.

Later chapters will reveal more information about the creation circles, but let's learn a bit more from the regressions about the ancient Lemurians' voyage to our planet, Earth.

CHAPTER 2
THE LEMURIANS' JOURNEY TO EARTH

As ancient Lemurians, we first came to Earth as fluid Beings of Light who could assume any body shape or form. Everything in our society was created from liquid Light. We came from the Source as Golden Light filtered through the Great Central Sun where we created form as Elohim or Lords of Light. The energy from the Great Central Sun was filtered again through the star systems. As highly evolved Beings of Light who had traveled beyond the Light, we were able to move through dimensions easily like we do now in our human form as we fly through the air in airplanes/gliders/jets/rockets, hang gliders, etc. We carried our consciousness to many different star systems, including Andromeda, Arcturus, Pleiades, Alpha Centuri, Orion, and also Venus, as we collected skills and knowledge from each system to use on Earth.

From Andromeda, we learned much about the technologies of creating energy from sound and light and the higher frequencies of mathematics and sacred geometry which underlie all the structures we created in Lemuria. We learned to transport ourselves through time and space by building light ships.

On Arcturus, we learned more about the use of color and sound for healing and energy balancing. There are many Arcturian ships around the earth at this time constantly monitoring and balancing the earth's energies, which are being disrupted by human unconsciousness.

On the Pleiades, we also learned more about the technologies of combining light with crystals—how to harness and focus light and to use it for manifestation and teleportation.

On Sirius, the home of the Temple of the Eternal Flame, the Christ Light that holds the frequencies of Immortality, we learned that the consciousness of the Cosmic Christ was being seeded on the Earth at that time and has continued to the present—and the future probably. Many of us came directly from Sirius to Earth with our friends, the dolphins and whales.

On Alpha Centauri, we found a very innocent and pure energy and learned to bring Pure Love into form. This energy from the fifth dimension and above was very difficult to maintain in our descent into third dimensional density, but we all have the codes for it in our DNA.

It wasn't a question of some of us being from the Pleiades and others from Sirius. We had all been on each of the star systems at different times, and some of us have a stronger affinity with one system than another. We traveled through all the systems in our galaxy on the way from the Great Central Sun to Mother Earth. We collected all the knowledge that we would need for our earthly life experiment. That knowledge is encoded in our DNA and available to us once our Light Codes have been activated.

Some of us came through the middle star in the belt of Orion. It is a portal to another universe that vibrates at a higher frequency than Earth. The portal's opening begins with the blue white light of the fifth dimension where all is Oneness.

In the beginning we were Beings of Pure White Light. We assumed the colors and frequencies of the many dimensional planes and frequencies through which we traveled. All of those memories have been dormant in our DNA and are waiting to be activated.

Our point of entry into this solar system on our way to Earth was through Venus's geometric crystalline light portal. This was a landing stage for all the different groups, including Cetaceans, to congregate from all the other star systems. We spent a long time in the love vibrations of Venus where we worked with our etheric bodies in the many Temples of Love. Many of us are unaware that we are still working in the dimensional temples there in our astral bodies during our dream states.

On Venus, we brought together all of the knowledge we had learned from the other star systems and harmonized it with Pure Love, the vibration of Venus. The whales helped us do this and are waiting now to help us to remember that we are Love.

A Galactic Pulsation

In the very beginning, we were a galactic pulsation, a point of galactic power. In groups we used creative techniques of combining color, form, and beauty. The galactic power point created a physical body around it. It created everything, including its own physicality. It was a soul choice to bring the Light into the third dimension.

We brought the Light into the physical, and now we are bringing the physical back to the Light. This was our choice for our soul's growth. We knew the Light, but we didn't know if we could bring it into density and still be Light, and so we travelled through the star systems gathering great knowing on our way to Earth.

CHAPTER 3
CRYSTAL CITIES, TEMPLES, AND GRIDS

As we noted briefly earlier, we first came down to Earth as Beings of Light and worked with the Light to create. Earth planet was mostly water then, so we came down into the oceans, the easiest medium for us to begin the experiment of taking on dense form. In the beginning our bodies were very fluid—made of liquid light. We built crystal cities with our minds and wove them from the fabric of light, which is the essence that we carry within us. We lived there in harmony, Love, and balance for eons of time. We breathed the cities into form together, and they sang. They sang the heart song that we carry within. Each one of us had our own note, our heart song; the crystal amplified that sound and wove it into form.

The Great Temple

Now let's add to the former information about the Great Temple and the work done there. The crystal cities had seven levels. At the highest level and frequency was the Great Temple, the most sacred place in the city, sitting under a domed, clear crystal roof from which a tall crystal spire pointed up directly to the heavens. There was a large entrance to the temple with crystal pillars and many steps. Huge doors twenty feet tall opened outward. Inside were marble floors, a domed ceiling, and much light coming through. The Great Temple's exterior shape was adapted by thought to whatever shape was needed for a particular purpose.

Different groups would come in and create whatever their segment needed. The temple could also change shape internally while remaining the same outside—always with our conscious co-operation with the building. The temple was full of any kind of light we desired, like many candles for a muted effect or sunlight for a bright, warm light, or light cells/panels—all part of our advanced technology.

At certain times when the tall crystal spire of the Great Temple was aligned with the Great Central Sun and the many star systems, the temple teams consisting of gridmasters would receive the energies and transmit them into the city energy grids to be accessed by other elements of our society. The energy left the Source as Pure Light. As it came down closer to denser levels, its codes and glyphs became more visible. They were in a language of Light, eons old going back as far as history can go. The gridmasters received the information as shapes/geometry, pictures/visions/glyphs, and/or sounds. Each gridmaster would receive an aspect, and the team would reassemble all the parts in the center of the circle. This was an ongoing process, so every aspect of life was receiving new blueprints for continuous improvement. This is similar to the current process of upgrading computer programs.

To do our work, we stood on a star grid on the floor of the Great Temple; the star had as many points as there were members of the team. Some were teams of twelve who stood on a twelve-pointed star; some were teams of nine standing on a nine-pointed star, etc., depending on the nature of the work and the energy that was coming in. These stars were the focal point of a grid, which then ran down to all the other levels of the city. We then programmed the new codes into the grids.

Each member of the team put the information into the star grid as it was received, and the star interconnected with all the other structures in the city.

The main grid underlying the entire city was Wholeness and Love. This was the basic grid, which ensured that every aspect of life and society was in harmony with the whole. In addition, each building had its own sacred geometry and received the energy of the whole—the Love vibration. Everything and everyone was connected to the whole through the main grid of Wholeness and Love as a unifying matrix. The gridmasters transmitted the information into the grids, which maintained and supported the city and all the activities in it and sent it to other cities' temple teams.

Aspects of the Outlying Temples' Circles

When the individuals in the other cities gathered in their temple co-creation circles, each circle downloaded information from the grids that was specific to their area of specialty. Each team had its own DNA code for activating a frequency, and each area, such as gardening, technology, healing, architecture, etc. These teams were adept at downloading and extracting codes for new ways of working in their areas of specialty. The teams received the new codes and passed them on to others in their area to create whatever was sent. For instance, they might create a new process to grow plants or a new way to create energy from crystals. Thus, multiple teams were involved with different aspects with no one team having the entire code.

When they extracted codes for their specialty areas, an individual might receive more than one aspect of the incoming blueprint: sound, visual, and/or geometry.

For example, someone might receive sound codes and visual codes while someone else might receive geometry and sound codes. Some downloads were brought in by teams of women only, so it would also be possible for a female to be part of a women-only team. There were also male-only teams, who worked with downloads that had more male energy involved. For example, a male-only team might work with architecture while a female-only team would download information on childbirth.

Another way the temple teams might access the codes would be in layered aspects that required different individuals in the circles to access different layers of information. The number of people picking up each area would depend upon the complexity of the blueprint. It was like a multi-layered matrix with geometries overlapping one another that could be broken down into different layers; for example, one person could receive the sound codes for layer 1, and another person would receive sound aspects for layer 2, while someone else would receive the visual aspects for layer 1, etc.

Some of the more complex blueprints required teams of twelve—usually six females and six males, but not always since there were also the female-only and male-only teams we spoke about earlier. Other combinations were possible, too. Simple blueprints might need a team of only three. If we stood in a team of twelve and drew lines of various patterns, we created geometric shapes. For example, if we connected either with the person opposite or next to us or the third person around the circle, we formed a triangle. The shape of the lines depended on the nature of the creation. Those opposite each other or on the points of the same triangle within a star had complementary energies and balanced one another.

Regardless of the aspects of the teams, all connected through the center of the circle, for it was there that all was jointed together in Oneness to be dispersed throughout the grids.

And so it is that individuals always participated in more than one team. An individual could be part of the healing team, a women- or men-only team, and the Great Temple team of gridmasters. It is essential to understand that everyone was acting as a separate unit on many levels.

New information and activations for the next level of consciousness would arrive when it was time for them to be accessed by others. In this way the new codes were being transmitted throughout the city, and people were absorbing them directly into their energy fields. We all hold the blueprint as part of ourselves and were born with the matrix of Wholeness. When the time is right, the archive which holds the templates of all creation can be accessed and certain fractions of the knowledge transmitted. There were teachers in all the different fields who were initiated to transmit specific parts to others.

The new energy added another frequency and dimension of the energy to the grids. Since the grids were the matrix that supported everything and the disseminators of the energies, their maintenance was essential. Specific individuals were devoted to this etherically, adjusting, adding, and deleting as it was needed. Physical work was not needed because everything was so vital and so light-filled that everything co-operated together in divine coordination.

The Creation of Light Bodies

First, we came in through the tall, crystal spire as our colors. In the beginning, we were in Light bodies, not physical bodies. The form for downloading more Light body images was waiting to be created was in the antenna. In order for more light bodies to be created, a spiraling energy would come down the antenna under the dome of the Great Temple. The energy was in a beautiful swirl of colors that twirled, radiating incredible colors. Our bodies were like spheres of Light: blue, pink, violet, lavender, magenta or gold. Under the dome, the antenna activated the Light body. Our Light bodies were fed from Source through the antenna. The temple teams were all swirling spheres of light, just being. We connected with each other in our consciousness and could interweave with each other, sharing our colors.

We were so much part of the whole that everyone's awareness encompassed everyone else's and we were never alone. We all wove in and out of each other and exchanged pure Love. We fed each other then passed on to the next one. Pale green, gold, pink, lavender, violet and blue, each gave their color to the other in one harmonious beautiful dance.

While the Great Temple was on the highest frequency level in the crystal cities, the lowest level was beneath the water and had many channels leading from the ocean to a beautiful pool of clear aqua blue water. Dolphins and whales would swim in and out, and so did we when we were taking dolphin form. Our bodies were liquid light, so assuming any shape we wanted was easy.

Over time, gradually the city took on more shape. The energy that came out of the colors and spheres generated a more defined body with hands and features.

Dolphin energies helped. Streams of light came down the spire full of glyphs which held the blueprints. We could select the blueprint we wanted and then focus our intention into it. Our shape became more triangular with a more defined head and body. We selected the blueprint and brought it into form by holding it in the colors that we were. We used our colors to create form. All members of the team contributed their own color and together created a form.

From Mer Beings to Dolphins

In the next phase we were denser in form and went from our light bodies in the crystal cites into the oceans as Mer Beings. We created cities under the ocean with arches, columns, and domes that looked like white marble. There were lots of plants in and around our cities, all very fluid under the water, all in motion. The structures were not solid; the Mer Beings were more like a sperm and an egg with entwined male and female energies, creating fluid structures that were imprinted into form by intention. They were created by the male and female spiraling together—the orange/gold/male energy and the pinkish/purple female energy. The Mer Beings had tails like fish but they were more translucent, ethereal. They worked with the dolphins visualizing the city together—a domed, columned city. They could shapeshift back and forth between dolphins and Mer Beings. They created together in a dancing, mating, spiraling, visualizing flow.

After that time the Mer Beings became dolphins looking for the shore. First, there was a crystal city made of Light, then the underwater city, and then the land came up from under the ocean.

17

The dolphins emerged from the water and created a human body. Our bodies were liquid light, so assuming any shape we wanted was easy. First, it had hands and feet, but a dolphin head because it was the dolphin's third eye that was creating all this from the dolphin galactic brain.

We created the first cities on land through intention focused through the third cye. There were lots of plants, half water and half earth. We were above the water, but the plants were more like underwater plants—between what sea life and plant life are now.

Assuming Physical Form

DNA strands continuously released light codes for each next stage of evolution. From here we moved into the stage that was in human form. With that came more physical structures, all part of evolution and life emerging. We had human hands, touch, and the ability to feel each other's faces. It totally changed everything, not so much the third eye creation, but now it was with human hands—a totally different experience. That was when we started building using our hands. We lost some of the beauty, the wondrousness. Touch changed things. Instead of just being and creating through thought and visualization, we now created using our hands with material rather than non-material energy. Now we had mortality; we had death. In this denser form, we were physical, but in the places before birth and after death, we were still on the ethereal planes where we moved and created by thought and intention.

At first we were only in the crystal cities on the ocean bottom because there wasn't much land. Later more land came up from underneath the ocean, so then we built cities on the land. Then we put the energy of the grids into the ley lines which network the whole earth. Points across the whole earth became receivers and transmitters so that the Grids of Wholeness enveloped the Earth and kept everything in balance and harmony. When the land came up from the water, we decided to take on dense bodies in order to walk on land. We used the crystal city's etheric blueprint for the land-based physical city. Then we used our minds to build cities and temples in those marble and stone cities.

The Temple as a Place of Reconnecting to Source

As in the crystal cities, now on land we came to the temple regularly to be reconnected to Source. We came from all different levels, especially if we had been traveling outside the city. Children were brought there to remember who they were. As before, the temple was the highest frequency of the whole city. Everybody had to come regularly so that they could maintain their frequency. Everyone was fed by the grid and by their pod (soul group that we came in with) connection. There wasn't so much a feeling of individuality as there is now on planet Earth. There never was a feeling of alienation and having to do everything alone. There were so many levels of support. We had our own pod and the group that we worked within that was a community. Then there was a greater community of everybody.

The Role of Water in the Temple

There was a fountain under a doomed roof in the middle of the inner temple, and water ran under the floor, so we were standing on the water as we worked in our circle teams. When the color in the temple changed, the color of the water changed as well and then went out into the ocean where it changed the frequency of the planet. If the temple was a heart, then the water that flowed was the arteries that picked up the energy of what we were doing so it could go out and feed the waters of the planet.

We were in tune with whatever was going on around the planet. When we saw things that needed shifting, we would work on the issue in the temple. Then the water would carry the necessary frequency to restore harmony and balance. That would change everything, even if what we needed to influence involved the land, for the water would evaporate into the sky and rain on that land.

The water also carried the frequency of the geometric shapes which could be invoked by whatever work we were doing. The combination of the water and the alchemical properties within its consciousness brought the frequency of the geometric shape with it. Then it would rain, and the water would get to wherever the work needed to be done.

Outside the temple, water ran underneath the streets—clean, clear water. There were waterways and gardens everywhere. The waterways had coverings so we could walk on them; however, if we wanted to touch the water, we could just put our hand through the cover. It was a protection for the water, yet at the same time we could have access to it.

Everything was so colorful and so beautiful. There was water everywhere; waterways were in geometric patterns like the spiral flower center of a chrysanthemum. There were spiral patterns all over the city.

The water carried life force through the city to feed everyone. It carried the frequency of everyone's love for everyone else; it was a symbiosis of earth, water, people, and plants. Living in this harmonious paradigm was so beautiful. All life forms fed and gave to each other. The plants would be put into a form that would enable them to transform into something else. There were no dumps for trash—no place where we threw things away. When we had finished with something, it transmuted into a new form.

The challenge for us now is to bring that memory into our physical bodies and to use more of our brain/third eye capacity. Since we moved into the lower chakras after The Fall, we only use a small percentage of our brain, and the rest has atrophied. We still have it as a potential, but now we have become so gross that we put it into the physical instead of being able to use the capacity that we have. This Aquarian Time is for us to be more creative in the mental right brain realm. As we reconnect our DNA strands, we will have the creative part of the brain again.

CHAPTER 4
MANIFESTING OUR WORLD

As we noted earlier, we created the cities and buildings in Lemuria from crystals and stones. In this chapter we will add to the information shared earlier about the Great Temple. The crystals in Lemuria were gargantuan, the size of houses and perfectly clear and smooth as if they had been cut with a diamond saw.

All the inhabitants were in a place of perfect trust with the Great Temple as the source of all the energy in the city. In the center of the Great Temple was a massive crystal which was the place of transmutation. It was of this dimension and yet not of this dimension—a portal that was here and not here—a doorway to the universe—its vastness and its power. This was where matter and energy met and co-mingled.

The Great Temple acted as an amplifier that radiated energy everywhere. It went all through the waterways and then into the oceans and to all the people in the city who added their vibration to it. Those who lived around the city amplified the energy because they were so inundated by the light all around them, so the whole city and countryside was steeped in this bliss energy. For everyone who lived in the city, it was like living in heaven and they shared that energy with the planet. Everybody was like a priest or priestess—so elevated and clear with that high frequency energy.

All Beings who worked in the Great Temple had to hang onto a sense of self because it was so easy to get swept into the vastness and literally disappear because the vortex was so expansive.

It was hard to be in that enormous power. There were other beings there assisting us from other dimensions. We were right on the edges, on the corners, holding the space, each one totally focused. It took immense concentration to maintain this balance between the letting go and the bringing in the energies. We were like beacons for this energy source. In one moment of not being focused, we could be swept away like in a wind. It was really intense, incredibly intense. It was where matter and energy and all the physical laws fuse into this other wave—like being at the center of the universe. Likewise, the priests and priestesses had to maintain their focus to bring the energy into this dimension and direct it to others.

As we stood there focused, we saw a strange light, like ultraviolet with other colors in it that came from black nothingness at the center which was the vastness of the void. Into this void came white light and from the white, it melded into the other colors of the spectrum as it entered the center of the temple. We escorted it and held it in balance. We were like the bridge between one another and other dimensions. We were all connected to God and had this perfect trust and power to create. We were the bridge to the vastness. We stood like sentries around the center near the walls, and this powerful energy came through us. We stood half-way between being human and being God in this vastness—half-way in it yet right at the edge. It was like being in a black hole where you are not sucked in but right at the edge where if you went any further, you would be sucked in and vaporized/destroyed.

When working in the Great Temple, we, this team of twelve beings standing on a twelve-pointed star, could have no ego. We stood on the edge, holding this incredible energy; it was almost too much.

We kept the dome in place; we drew the energy through ourselves, which took deep concentration. We kept it right on the edge of bringing it in and letting it out, between the in-breath and the out-breath, and all the heavens moved into place, the stars, and the planets. There was a moment when we drew it all in and released it, and it flowed into the grids. It came down through our bodies into the Earth on the vertical plane and on the horizontal plane into a grid of light that went from the Temple all around the world.

It was particularly powerful in the city, but it was transmitted everywhere and there were no boundaries. This was a place beyond physical boundaries. The energies were transmitted to the others in the rest of the world in complete unity—all were part of this culture, not just those in the Great Temple. It was the power source. We were the conductors; we manipulated raw power beyond this dimension where physical laws meld and blended it into other forms.

It is truly beyond the ability of Man and our current consciousness to comprehend the enormous power of this, to bring that into human consciousness and to transmit it so that it can be received by others. It lifted up the consciousness of everyone—so wonderful! It made every Being in the temple like a super being, like ascended masters, being able to transmit matter and to create from nothing simply by focusing, creating intention, and then manifesting it in absolute perfection. We brought it in, held it, stabilized it, and put it into the grid, then were allowed to rest as others came in to replace us.

It is difficult for us now to conceptualize how it was there— only because those Beings were absolutely connected so completely to God consciousness, to the Oneness of everything.

The creation of these physical forms brought a sense of Bliss, Oneness, Love, and connection to all others. The forms were brought forth from a place where there was no past, present or future—only One. We brought what will be to what is. All that will be and All That Is and All that was are in this place simultaneously. We brought the Divine in all of its dimensions.

We brought in the perfection that included the ability to be in spirit and in union with the vastness while at the same time to have this intelligence, which was not separate or individual thinking. It was like turning into Light, very peaceful yet ecstatic union, bliss. This was the raw energy that we took and we crafted. There were others like us standing on other special sites all around the world, receiving it and passing it on.

The female drew down the feminine aspect of the codes in the blueprint, which perfectly matched the masculine aspects of the codes. Streams of codes flowed through polarity partners, which matched the codes their counterpart was bringing in. The fusion of the two partners ignited these codes. This energy was beamed out from the pair and passed onto all the Lightworkers throughout the grid.

People were coming and going from the temples to power points all over the Earth. They arrived, received the codes, downloaded the information from the codes, and then gave back energy to the grid themselves. Thus they became emissaries of Light as they walked upon the Earth. Little filaments of Light connected them to the grid as they wandered about so everybody was connected to the energy. Some were connected with multiple points—others with only one point. Everyone who was walking upon the Earth at that time was connected to this energy, the path back to the Source.

We fed each other. We were pure Love, and our essence was passed on through the beams of light which we projected into the grid, maintaining it with our light. Streams of codes came in as we stood under the beam. We stood with our palms touching, creating intense energy. All of these codes were stored in our DNA and are now waiting to be activated. The male and female came together, merging and fusing their DNA. The female held the codes for the feminine aspect of creation, and the male held the codes for the masculine aspect of creation. We put them together, merging the spiral helix of the DNA and downloading this energy into the grids. When others came in to take over, we would pass the flow to them. They walked into us and we walked out of them, in order to maintain the continual flow. There always had to be someone in the flow to hold the energy, but we also we carried that energy with us as we traveled.

Now we must bring this energy here to the Earth plane to anchor it into the crystalline heart of Gaia and into the Earth grids. We can step back in time to get the codes and step forward to bring them here now. The codes light up the crystal grid of Gaia. The team in the temple holds the beam and feeds it to us to bring it here now. The beam of galactic energy from Source goes down into the center of the Earth and explodes into starlight as Gaia births it into her star body now. We connect the energy from Source through the temple team as they flow their hearts into us, and we flow that energy into the grid—in our present time. We stand on Earth now just as we did in the Lemurian temple, holding the energy right on the edge. It is so powerful. Like before, we hold it at the point of balance between bringing it in and letting it out while it goes into the grids.

CHAPTER 5
CONSTRUCTING BUILDINGS IN LEMURIA

Those Lemurians who were able to go into the archives and download the matrix for the structure coordinated the creation of a building. They were initiated to bring in the matrix because they were tested on their ability to receive without distortion so they were able to get a perfect blueprint for the building. They would then transmit parts of the blueprint to the people who were going to make it.

There were people who were responsible for building the physical aspects and those who were working with the energetic qualities of the creation of a building. Specific templates existed for each. The one that downloaded the blueprint information transmitted this information separately to each of the other members of the building team.

The frequency, the shape, the color of a building had to be in alignment with the concept of Wholeness of that building since the building had a consciousness. Otherwise, the building would be a combination of individual efforts. Even though people had different functions within it, the concept of Wholeness was the unifying principle.

A ceremony or at least a conscious moment was included in the building process to keep all thoughts, actions and intentions in alignment with the concept of Wholeness of that building. All would monitor their own input to make sure they were keeping in alignment with that Wholeness. There were also people who would monitor the building to make sure that it was in the concept of the Wholeness of the city.

They were the over-viewers of the more energetic connections so that every facet of what was manifesting would be a reflection of the Wholeness that was coming in through the codes.

In addition, a temple team would be assembled for the particular creation that was going to be manifested. They stood upon a geometric shape, which had the same number of points as the team. Each project had a specific geometry, and by getting into that geometry, they would stay in contact with the Wholeness for their specific creation. The team could be 3, 6, 7, 8, 9, or 12 members, depending on what was being created. They would stand in their places in the geometry, such as the points of a star or the sides of a hexagon or octagon.

Different geometric shapes emitted different frequencies, so their use depended on the purpose of the building. There could be several buildings of the same shape if there was a lot of work to be done in that aspect. Rooms would be a certain shape, but over time when that part of the work in those buildings was complete and that energy wasn't needed anymore, the building would morph into a different shape. The building picked up on all the energy around it and would change its shape to match the frequency that was being emitted by the city. If we were working on one particular aspect, we would focus on the next shape, and the building would morph into it. Buildings were constantly being adapted to what was needed at the time. All the structures were like living entities which water held together and helped change into the new form. The structure was always fluid, always in a state of readiness to be whatever was needed next.

The team used sound, intention, and visualization. All focused through the third eye, and whatever they were focusing on actually manifested in the center of the design. In essence the building material was the same for everything—liquid light in all its varieties, including crystals/crystallized. It came in as light, which was focused and densified into form. The buildings had a translucent quality because they were made from liquid light. They had softness to them and radiated light. We were able to build huge structures like the pyramids by singing into the material so that it became soft and could be molded. Some people were adept at toning buildings and structures into being.

The blueprint for the building was connected with the purpose of the building. There was always the Wholeness grid underlying the grids for the specific purpose or qualities of the building. A building would have its own specific grid related to its purpose, such as healing, but that grid would be on top of the Wholeness grid.

Building was done when the energies were very clear. It was a co-creative process with the consciousness of the liquid light and the team, organically growing a building. We directed and built it with our minds molding the crystalline structure and holding the consciousness while we worked in rotation because there needed to be someone at the site the entire time.

Special seed crystals were grown whose purpose was to expand and grow at an accelerated rate. We would hold the thought of what we wanted to create in our minds, construct it on the etheric plane, and then attune ourselves to the crystals. Our thoughts would come into symbiotic connection with the crystal, be downloaded into it, and the crystal would manifest our thoughts in the form of a building. These were very specialized crystals created for this purpose.

31

The crystal was different than the kind of crystal on Earth today. It was more resilient and had the ability to change form as needed. It would communicate back to the team as it was growing, so it was like a mandala. Water was part of the construction as the binding agent that brought everything together. The crystal would feed back ideas that would fine-tune the plan, thus creating a better building as the crystal and water contributed their intelligences to the team during their creative process. The crystal and the water grew and worked together so that the building grew fast. This co-creative fluidity of communication and form with water as the binding agent was alive, growing, and interactive. The walls formed from the combination of crystal and water.

There were different densities in a building. For instance, floors had a higher density than walls. The floor was created as a reflection of the Wholeness grid; it had the same imprint so that with each step we took, we connected with the whole. It had the same colors and the same grid pattern in it.

Once the building was created and in use, if we needed it to be a different shape or color we could interact with it and it would change to whatever we needed. The colors of the buildings could also change depending on the kind of work we needed to do. We stood in our temple teams in a circle, toning different tones based on our agreed intent before we started and the communication of the building itself. It created an extraordinarily powerful wave of frequency that went right around the planet. It was amazing what a small number of people could create with the combination of all our energy in symbiosis with the water, crystals, light, everything. It all worked together.

The city was laid out in a circular pattern like a mandala. Everything was geometrically planned around circular streets. There were rings of streets with buildings between them. The whole city was conceived beforehand in a master plan. The builders would go out with their crystals, attune themselves to the crystals, and then carry out their part of the project. Building started at the center of the circle and worked outwards in ever widening circles. Each circle was complete in and of itself. The construction going on was always in the outer ring, but the city within was already established. As the circles were completed, the city became more established in a larger context.

Later on in the Lemurian civilization, the buildings were shorter than in the original crystalline cities of light. They were squatter, between six and ten stories high. In the early ones, we could see light through them, but the later ones were more opaque, more utilitarian than aesthetic.

CHAPTER 6
TECHNOLOGY

This was how Lemuria was about 70,000 years ago. We were the pioneers, living here while observing how things evolved so that we could find the best way to function on this plane. We needed to be in the energy of Earth for a while to see what worked best.

Water ran underneath the streets in Lemuria and created an energy field, which interacted with vehicles. The energy carried in the water radiated above the streets so that cars were able to interact with it—rather like a magnetic train where the cars never touch the ground. The vehicles were two-person crafts, like little spaceships that rode on a cushion of air. When we got to our destination, we turned the car off, and it settled down. When the field collapsed, the car floated gently down to the ground, the wings folded up, and we climbed out.

Larger vehicles were used to transport cargo. They were not as big as our trucks of today and were fairly small so that they could get in and out of the city without causing congestion. The transport vehicles were unloaded at the docks situated at higher levels than everything else. A switch activated the energy field and lifted the vehicle up. All the unloading docks were above street level, so the traffic could go right underneath them. The planners created different levels to allow free movement.

The goods came into an entrance lobby area. The offices, distribution, and storage areas were one story above this level and were reached by an elevator. Everything worked in harmony.

Each item of cargo had a field around it, so when a vehicle pulled up to a building, the receiving machinery attuned itself to whatever needed unloading first. The probe went in and let the cargo know what it needed to achieve the unloading. A weightless field was created, and everything unloaded automatically. The driver pulled the vehicle into the bay and waited until the light came on. Then he knew he was ready to go on to the next one, and the cargo floated out.

There was a chip on the outside of each package that created a field of intelligence around it so that when the package came in, the vehicle could interact with that intelligence. It knew exactly what it needed, the order it needed to be unloaded in, and where it needed to go. This intelligence was programmed in so workers didn't need to do any menial work.

The packages contained equipment for the offices and control centers. As businesses expanded and required new equipment, it was added onto existing machines. Technology was always updating itself. As it did, new things were transported in to upgrade what we already had. Everything was designed to be added to so that nothing was obsolete until a whole new paradigm came along. When that happened, there was always a way to recycle whatever had to be replaced.

Everything was built consciously, so there wasn't any trash. Everything was used. Things that were decomposing went into other things that used the energy of decomposition to create energy, like now we harness methane gas from landfill sites. Nothing went to waste in Lemuria. When something became obsolete, it would be used to serve another purpose. This is something we need to be doing now on Earth.

The manufacturing process was a co-creative process where things organically built themselves. When the co-creators came up with a design, they put a new program into the crystal, and it would automatically create the design. Robotics did the manual part of anything if it needed to be done. They were controlled by telepathy and were connected consciously to the crystals and the people who designed them. The robots came from off-planet.

Nobody needed to toil. If we needed something, we just made a request, and it arrived. We were in touch with our stellar roots which provided us with a constant exchange of information. Our technology came from other civilizations that were more advanced than we were, so we could spend more time "being" than "doing." Some of us were here from other star systems as technicians, monitoring the planet and evolving ourselves by being of service to the Lemurians.

CHAPTER 7
WORK

Everybody worked in a team which might also include the Temple Teams of priests and priestesses, along with the gardeners, teachers, healers, builders and technological researchers. Much of the work revolved around creating and maintaining everything by using subtle bodies rather than physical work. People were either creating new things or monitoring what had already been created. Society was not work-driven because there was a prevalent feeling of joy in serving the whole. On Earth today we are like worker ants; in the days of Lemuria, it was the machines that were the ants.

Most people were the equivalent of our highly paid executives. They had workout rooms and very comfortable surroundings in an environment that was conducive to people's happiness and well-being. The primary point of focus in designing something was that it should be effortless to operate. The next focus was that everything would be healthy for everyone and not emit any toxic fields. The final focus was that everything would be able to serve another purpose after its useful life had expired.

All of the work places were not really like going to work. People went to monitor things in a work environment where we could work on ourselves at the same time. Everything was designed for the well-being of everything and everybody. There were beautiful parks and gardens to walk in or to look at all throughout the city. People volunteered to work in the areas where their natural gifts lead them and where they would feel joy. Everyone believed there was no sense of work being a burden as everybody just did what they loved to do.

CHAPTER 8
SACRED UNION

The purpose of Sacred Union was to attain a higher state of unity consciousness. It was used as a way to transform energy. There was exquisiteness about it; the aim was to bring each partner more fully into connection with the Oneness. Couples of similar vibration were attracted to each other. There was intense passion, and they felt they had a similarity of interest, drive, purpose and connection. They were similar to us in that they were drawn to each other by passion, magnetism, and soul connection. They came together to balance male/female energies in an experience of Unity.

Couples came together in ceremony and passion to experience a greater Love by merging their individual love into a greater whole. In the beginning, it was more an energetic exchange, but as our bodies became denser, it became sexual although the union was always considered sacred, greatly honored, and revered. It was a celebration of the male and female energies coming together in perfect balance. Through ecstatic sacred union with The Beloved (soul partner), we could experience the ecstatic connection to The One, to Source on a deeper, passionate, intimate level.

A man and a woman would choose to come together to offer themselves as sacred vessels for Union with The Divine. This sacred Union was considered to be the highest form of service to create a chalice for the Sacred Feminine and a chalice for the Sacred Masculine. Through that union, those involved would literally bring The Divine into the energy field of the whole city. At first the energy would be fed into the cities' gridworks, but later it went into the grids of the whole earth.

The energy contained the two polarities of the God Field: male and female in a balanced form.

At all times, the purpose of the Union was to create a vehicle for Pure Love to be brought to Earth. This was one way in which we maintained the grids of Wholeness and Pure Love. It was a great honor to be invited into Union and to make The Great Marriage, which was the highest honor anyone could offer to another. When we brought the energy of Union down into the physical, it was very pure and sacred, so the Marriage rites were always performed in the Great Temple. It felt like a privilege to be able to bring that as an offering to the community for the grids.

After The Fall, the energies became distorted and the goal became physical pleasure, which was never the original intention. The Joy of Union is the essence of the Tantric teachings which Hindu and Tibetan schools still teach. When we came together in Sacred Union, we connected at all seven chakras, and our light bodies merged. The male had his own matrix, and the female had her own matrix. When these two matrices merged, they wove through each other and created a whole new geometry, a new creation of form from liquid light.

Contact was first made through the eyes. For each couple, there was a specific sequence of sounds, colors, tones, and breaths that connected the chakras and transformed the connection into an energetic light experience. The merging of their two light bodies in ecstatic union created an incredible energy field. It was a total surrender to the energy of Wholeness. It looked like infinite expansion, the creation of a sphere, which grew into a vortex. There was a huge energy build-up in the sphere which was exquisite on the personal level and could be focused for the creation of any project.

It could be fed into the Wholeness matrix to sustain the Wholeness field of everything. It could also be focused into the creation of a child or used in the manifestation of anything that the couple needed/desired to bring into form.

Everyone in union had the capacity to reach a phase of total Wholeness, but some were more gifted in generating more energy for the vortex than others. They were like the energy batteries for the Wholeness/Love field—they kept the fires burning. They were the ones who had received more initiations to help them access the Archives and to bring in more power. There was a natural ebb and flow in knowing when the fields needed to be "charged" in this way. Both partners had the awareness of when the field needed to be sustained.

The purpose of Sacred Union was rarely to create children, per se. Instead, it was to feed the Love energy to the system as it was the most powerful energy that we could create. At the moment of ecstatic union, the energy automatically connected to the field. We didn't have to "do" anything to connect the energy, just have the intention to feed it into the system, like acupuncture points, into the grid.

Sacred Union was the true purpose of the sexual rites in their purest form as practiced in many ancient religions. The energy created by union of the sacred masculine with the sacred feminine into one holy union could be directed for healing or for bringing the power of creation into a project by holding that purpose as a focus or intention. The druids used this energy to assist crops to grow and to keep all the kingdoms in balance. Ancient Egyptians and Native Americans used the sexual rites to create high frequency energy for initiating students.

The true purpose of Tantra is to experience the Divine through ecstatic union. After The Fall, sexual energy became desecrated, and the temple priestesses were held in slavery and prostitution. It is now time for sexual energy to be returned to the temple where it becomes a vehicle for the experience of pure and holy Love.

We are reconnecting at this time with the partners we worked with in Lemuria. We already have the codes for ecstatic union within our energy bodies waiting to be reactivated. We are connecting with our partners of old. When we connect with them and share our energies, we call it "making love." We are the Love and when we join together in Bliss, in orgasmic Joy, we are aware that all Beings are in partnership with us: dolphins, whales, stars, trees, and elementals.

Now we are learning not to exclude anyone anymore. We are beginning to forget to say "No" and to remember to say "Yes."

Every thought, every image, every possibility we can think of—all become one joyous vibration pervading everything and uniting everything at the same time. Then we realize that All is One and All there is, is One.

CHAPTER 9
BABIES/CHILDREN

Preparation to Welcome a Soul

The whole community decided upon whether a child/a child's soul could be part of that society. They had to make a unanimous choice to accept that being. The child's soul would ask to be a part of that society, and the council would gather to agree whether or not to accept that soul. Thus, the birth of a child was a conscious co-creation by parents, the child, and the community as a whole.

Once it was decided who the parents and the child were to be, a ceremony was performed to create the child. When they were creating the child, everyone involved connected with the new being as light essence with the soul of the child. The frequencies of the male and female energies would harmonize with that of the child. The child knew where it was going and the community knew who was coming.

The couple who decided to bring forth a new life would spend a lot of time in the temple preparing themselves to be vehicles for creating that new life. It was a very serious commitment, and they spent a lot of time realigning themselves with purity and innocence. They had to be a very pure vessel to bring in a new soul. The parents spent a lot of time connecting to the Love, examining themselves as to their motivation and intention, aligning themselves with Love, and emptying themselves of ego so that they could be a pure vessel for the new life form.

In the beginning, the female and male energy and that of the child would all blend their essences together as light before they started to create the physical vehicle for the child to embody, ensuring that the combination was suitable. Throughout this, a group of people toned into the center point of the circle to support the unique combination of the individuals involved. In addition, there were people who would monitor the process to determine if the parents and children were going to be in vibrational harmony. The monitors saw the colors in the energy fields of all three entities and observed what happened when they came together. If their frequencies didn't match energetically, they didn't go through with the birth.

Creation of a Soul

If the frequencies matched, the child was created in unity consciousness with the parents coming together as one. To create the child, male and female entities would come together and join energies at the crown, heart, and sacral chakras. They would use sound to tone the child into being. The couple would join hands to create an energy flow between their hearts. They would focus the Love energy through conscious awareness to create the child. They used the breath to build the energy, breathing love into each other, and creating the child between them. The parents connected all their chakras, merging their light bodies. The two matrices of the male and the female moved in and through one another and from that merging, a totally new geometry was formed. One matrix moved through the other, merging and creating a new matrix, a new geometry.

The child was created by densifying liquid light; the densification went according to the individual geometries, so the geometry that was formed was a synthesis of both the man and the woman. They were co-creators and the densification of the new being would align with the geometry that was created in the merging union.

There was a difference in the intricacies of the geometries of different people. Some would have simple geometries while others were more complicated. For example, teachers would have different geometries than students. There was no judgment in this; it was just a matter of holding more information. People would have different colors in their fields, and when we looked deeper, we would see the differences in the geometry that showed themselves as the golden base of the Beings. Of course, there would be a difference in complexity of the geometry and in the division of the colors.

A lot was involved in the creation process of carrying a child. At first it was not a pregnancy as we know it where the female physically carries the child. It was more about holding the child energetically as it developed. This was a time when the qualities of the child were being infused or downloaded. It was being held in a sacred space between two people. Both parents joined as one with the child held at the center between them. Each one would be feeding the child either masculine or feminine qualities, each being responsible for a particular role in the co-creation of the child.

During the time of creating the child, the parents didn't do anything else. They were not distracted by other aspects of life. It was as if they went to a special place because this was their job: to be conscious co-creators of the technologies, virtues, and qualities that this new being would embody.

They needed to be present for this child completely. The parents were supported by a group of people around them, feeding energy into them. The birthing circle team would change shifts, but the parents remained in a state of sacred union during the whole time of creating this child which took many months in our time.

Birth

During that time both parents continued connecting their chakras and focusing the energy through the hearts. The heart energy continued to expand to create a space for the child to develop. He was infused with love until the space could no longer contain him, not birth as we know it. It was more like a pod developing in the heart space between two people. As the heart expanded, the pod opened and the child was born. The pod could no longer contain him because his being-ness was so filled with love that he emerged from the pod.

Post Birth

After the birth, the team welcomed the child by putting the little one into a ceremonial bath with holy water. The parents were prepared ceremonially to receive their child, and this ritual helped the child to come into the body softly so that the soul would not be in shock. There was a great amount of heart energy as he was surrounded by warmth, touch, holding, singing, nurturing, joy, gentleness and sweetness. Every child was welcomed in this way. It was so different from the way babies come in now in hospitals and wards and bright lights.

When the child was born, a team of helpers would sing to the child and hold it continuously while the parents rested and restored themselves or did something else, knowing that the child would be cared for. Shifts of people took turns rocking, holding, loving, and feeding the baby. The little one was fed more with energy than with physical food. The caring team would hold the child to their hearts, and the child would be infused with sweetness and with the specific colors of the caregiver.

Everyone had a role in this process but not just for the birth. The whole community and specifically the birth team and parents were involved in the process of inviting the soul of the child to come in, helping to grow the body and integrate it into the community.

In the early Lemurian time when we were more ethereal, everything was vibration and color. As a new being was born, it was carried to all the different zones and frequencies that the different people had as their specialties. Each area was a different color, so as the new soul was taken to each of them and held, the child would receive as much of that color/those colors from the person or group as was needed. In time, the color of the child would become obvious, and he would be channeled into serving in that area.

This way of Love has been forgotten now. In Lemuria, every child was received in the same loving way as part of the community, which helped the child to remember the focus of Love. They didn't want to rush things so they could get on to the next one as they do now.

Birthing was a job and a lot of work, but it was done with love, joy, and reverence.

The community decided together to receive the child, even though the parents birthed it, as it would become a member of the community. There was no "possession" of the child like today where we belong to certain parents and family. The focus was more communal and universal than individual, more about community. Even for the parents, it wasn't personal. It was a special privilege to bring a particular child or entity into being, but that didn't mean that the child "belonged" to them. They would perhaps have a special role with overseeing the development of this particular little being, but it was a community effort and everyone was cared for equally.

CHAPTER 10
EDUCATION AND CHILD DEVELOPMENT

Children were taught how to stay connected to the light. They had practice sessions of bringing the light down and in. Children were born from the light and stayed with it until they got older, and then they needed regular sessions of meditation to sit with the light. They would come to the Great Temple and sit in the colors of the light, golden light, and pillars of light. Here they would be infused with light as they sat in it, knowing it, and being it. The light came down from the sun through the spire and the crystal roof of the temple.

Children were taught how to work with their inner resources, to know what those resources were, and how to harness and develop them. All children were taught that they were part of the light and how to tap into their hearts to make decisions and to check in with how they were feeling, how to work with energies, and how to take care of themselves. As they developed, they were taught how to monitor thoughts and emotions to feel whatever it was they needed to experience and how to transform themselves with Love.

Before The Fall there was no pain. Children were taught how to stay in balance, how to work with the colors of each chakra, and how to work with their power and intuition. All of this was taught and known as innate abilities. They learned which colors related to which chakra and how to use these colors and the energy of each. Children were taught how to check in with themselves, to feel where in their body they were experiencing a sensation, and how to live their lives in Love.

They were shown how to nurture, comfort, and care for themselves by staying connected to Source.

Some children's abilities would be known ahead of time; for others, when their abilities became apparent, they would be placed with the members of the community who could nurture them and their particular gifts or areas of interest. Schooling would always be with different people teaching different things. At a certain age they would be with one group, then at another age with another group. They didn't go to school as our society does. They would move from group to group. The first group did the program for baby development, and after that, they went to each section of the community. Children began to specialize in their own particular area of expertise as they grew older. It was similar to what we do here but more of a group setting like in the Waldorf schools. They would learn the basic level of each specialty with the group they were growing up with, but the focus was always on community and Love.

Children lived in the community area where they were currently being taught; each place had everything they needed. They had a sense of belonging, purpose, and direction. All their needs were met, and they were valued as an integral member of the whole. As the child moved through the different areas, the color of the child would become obvious and he would be channeled into working in that area. Some worked with energies, some with sound, and some created form. Everyone had a place. Each area had a predominant color. The healers tended to work with the violet ray; the energy people worked with blue. Each child received all colors but each had a resonance that would become predominant, the one that was its own color. The teachers would then know that was the area the child needed to receive more activations.

Each group had its own color. Some of its purpose was to work with the children to take them through a series of activations to see where their abilities flowed most easily. Some members of each group would be doing the work of the specialty while others would be teaching that specialty within the temples. This was when we were in more subtle bodies and our buildings were more ethereal. Later on we did the same thing but within marble halls and structures.

The children would travel together in groups—the group or pod they came in with. Children came in waves. There would be a group of children coming in at one time, like a soul group. That group stayed together and traveled together at all times to all the different areas, such as gardening, technology, or healing. They would go to the teaching aspect of each area to receive teaching, always with love, gentleness, and encouragement. There was no judgment, no differentiation between success and failure. No one was judged or graded. It was only noted that if a specialty came more easily or with more difficulty, then they would be channeled on to the next level of that specialty.

There were many levels within each facility. Everyone was given a basic grounding. For instance, in the plant realm everyone was shown the dynamics of energy flows, the resonances which all plants needed. There was a basic grid that sustained all plants. Then as the plant became more specialized, there were layers of that basic grid that would be more suited to the specialized needs of particular plants. All children would be given a basic knowledge of how plant life energy worked, and then those who showed more aptitude for that work were given the higher, more refined, specialized knowledge in that area as the others moved on to their next place.

Nobody was ever made to feel less than anyone else. There was no kind of hierarchy. It was just a matter of all being encouraged to find out where their heart, their joy and their love was, where their gifts could be most beneficial to the community, and where they could be of most service. Everyone was pleased to be of service. We all knew we were here to serve and that by serving others, we serve the One and ourselves.

When we found the vehicle for service which flowed most naturally for us, we were overjoyed. It was an expression of our basic light, color, and essence that served the whole community. We were joyful, smiling, laughing and playing. Work was not a burden and didn't feel like "work" because we felt so connected and supported.

Much of the education was by direct transmission of codes from the teacher to the students. We absorbed the energy or activation by moving through the energy field of the person transmitting a certain color or frequency. Some people would be monitoring the energy field of the students to read their energies and their colors to find out what their gifts were. This would show them which color codes the student would be able to transmit most powerfully.

Deep violet in the energy field was the highest concept, including Love and Oneness. Amethyst represented compassion. Pink was the connection to the angelic planes, being very closely associated with the purple energy. Light gold represented joy, fun, and movement in the body, like dancing, as well as assimilation and absorption. Light gold was also about interaction between different beings in a joyful dance, working with each other's energies as a form of communication.

Green, like a pale emerald, signified connection to the plant kingdom.

People were constantly being monitored to be able to keep in balance. All had a gift, the color they were most powerful with, but they also needed to stay in balance with all the other colors. The students would go to people who taught them in their strengths and people who monitored their balance overall. This meant that they had to have all the colors represented in a balanced way to be able to teach or to perform service from a place of Wholeness.

It was individualization within the Wholeness, and all contributed their gifts to that. People were monitored for their gifts at a very young age but not in a harsh way. At some point they would be initiated to allow them to teach whatever their strengths were. This was an activation or an official strengthening of their connection with one particular archive.

The archive had Wholeness within itself, so the people stayed connected to the Wholeness even if they only taught part of it. It was not like it is today in science where everyone has their own area. There was always a consciousness of the whole and its facets and what it means to be whole and to be within the whole.

Everyone received a foundation of the concept of Wholeness in order to understand the part for which they were being trained and what it meant inside the whole intricate web. A base knowledge of the Wholeness of the web was taught, as well as the activation and reinforcement of their personal gifts.

Children were born with the matrix of Wholeness, all the colors. They needed opening up gently and playfully.

They didn't need to be trained into Wholeness because it was already within them. The opening was not automatic, so a certain frequency was needed to allow children to open to their Wholeness. By moving into other people's energetic bubbles, their own frequencies were activated. Their basic matrix of Wholeness was gently and automatically opened up by hearing toning and meeting other people with their specific color coding.

Over time, as the energies sank lower into density, the matrix couldn't be opened up anymore and the basic matrix of Wholeness became unavailable. The frequencies lowered, and people didn't radiate completeness in their color bubbles anymore. This was the time of The Fall.

After The Fall, children were no longer opened up to Wholeness. Anyone can put knowledge on top and push it into the system, but if it doesn't have a receiver that is connected to Wholeness, the end result will be fragmented knowledge like we have in science now. We no longer work from the consciousness field of Wholeness. Nobody is to be blamed; the field just isn't open anymore.

CHAPTER 11
COUNCILS AND HOW
DECISIONS WERE MADE

Decisions which affected the whole group were made by a council which would meet in the Great Temple sitting around a table. The council consisted of representatives from every aspect of society: healing community, gardening, waterways, technology, animals, and temple overseers. The council would meet whenever there was a need. There were regular times to meet, but there was also agreement that anyone could call a meeting if it was needed. The meeting would continue until the inquiry was resolved and brought to a peaceful, agreeable resolution that worked for the highest good of all. They always kept their focus. There was never a question of not keeping the focus, and the focus was Love. There was no temptation to stray from that. It was a perfectly functioning society.

Each meeting began with a prayer which was the same each time. They asked to remember their focus of Love, community, and co-operation. There wasn't a leader as such because each one was a representative from a section of the community. Time was allowed for each representative of each area to speak. The person who called the meeting would begin by stating that their area was experiencing something that was a challenge and/or needed a new way of looking at a situation. They asked for input from all the other groups. Then everyone would know what was going on in the other segments of the community, and everyone was in the light of truth.

There were also mediators who sat in on all the meetings of both the community as a whole and of the individual areas of specialty. They always held the focus of the highest good of all to ensure that any suggestions or solutions were in alignment with the overall design and concept of Love and Wholeness for the whole community. There was no sense of power struggles or antagonistic groups trying to force a decision which favored them, just awareness of the good of the Whole.

CHAPTER 12
GARDENS

The first gardens were created by thought. There was no soil, and everything was created out of the ethers by thought. The forms changed all the time depending on what we wanted to see. Even if we were in a different location than the garden, we could create what we wanted, and it would be there before us; and we could change it if we wanted something else. The gardens were used for healing and energizing people. No one was ever sick then because we had this energy constantly around us. If we wanted something, we could create it around us, whether it was a rainbow, flowers, a waterfall with colors, beautiful birds, or lights of colors. We just thought it into being, and it manifested right before our eyes.

In the beginning everything was liquid light, including the growing food and us. We created the fruits and vegetables in our minds and simply replaced what we had picked with our focused intent. We brought the seeds from other dimensions. In early Lemuria, plants and gardens were everywhere. The whole city was a garden. There were gardens and water all around; it was artistry.

Later, as we increased in density, the plants became more physical like the fruits and vegetables we have now; they became greener like our leafy greens and vegetables. This made the difference between the physical manifestation and the original matrix of Wholeness greater, so there was more chance of distortions. As the frequency lowered, it was increasingly difficult to retain memory of the basic Wholeness matrix.

Later when we were in physical bodies, we had gardens that were very lush with tropical plants and huge flowers with vibrant colors.

Creation at the Lemurian Temple at Glastonbury Abbey Site in England

The ruins of the Glastonbury Abbey in England today were once the site of a huge open-air temple with Grecian columns, a beautiful floor, and beautiful designs. It was here where we materialized object as four archangels stood at the four corners. In the center was a great central clear quartz altar that twelve young Lemurian women, pure of form and heart, sat around as they held hands. As they watched the altar, they would materialize an object in midair above it. The object was egg-shaped and liquid like shiny, metallic silvery shimmering moving light. It had color and form around it. They breathed together and began to observe a bluebell emerging as if it had been birthed from the egg-shaped object; roots, leaves, shoots and flowers appeared. It was their intention created from their thoughts which manifested the bluebell.

They held the blueprints from the devas and archangels in their minds. Each of the twelve brought in a different aspect: sound codes, light codes, and geometries. One would obtain the design and then project it to the others through mental telepathy. Then all would all project it into the egg, and it would manifest physically. The egg was luminous, translucent, and liquid; it was in this world and not in it at the same time. It was a portal.

Others worked with the consciousness of the rocks and soil and activated the energy in the stones of the earth.

Sound was used for this activation, combined with intention. People worked in teams, toning into the plants and helping them to grow. We used different tones in different places in conjunction with external conditions. For instance, we would tone during electrical storms or the phase of the moon to focus the energies. We worked with the plants, the stars, and the cycles of the earth in co-creation. We had teams who possessed the knowledge of planetary positions and cycles and the appropriate tones.

The Role of Service in the Community

People could choose if they wanted to offer their services in the growing aspects of the community; such as watering, weeding, planting or harvesting. There was enough for everyone to do, so all could do whatever they felt drawn to. The gardens surrounded the city, and the buildings surrounded the big courtyards in the middle, all connected by the lines of communication between the different areas of activity, with each other and the gardens.

We grew all kinds of vegetables, including cabbages, carrots and tomatoes, as well as flowers and orchards full of different fruits. We also had animals—cows, chickens, goats, and sheep. We didn't eat the animals; we just used their produce of milk, eggs, and wool. The animals each had a role, and they knew what it was, such as sheep offering their wool for clothing. Each animal had a sacred job and was held in sacred regard as if they were human. They weren't treated any less than human. They were included as part of the sacredness of life that everybody lived.

Animals were considered as part of the bigger picture, of creation, the greater whole where all worked in harmony. We helped the plants to grow through love. The people with this role sat with the various vegetables. The gardeners would sit with a certain vegetable as if it were a baby and give it Love vibrations. Each person had the freedom to choose his or her own particular expression of this vibration, which could be toning, singing, praying or projecting colors.

The purpose of every member of society was to serve. Therefore, all chose what they wanted to do or focus on. For instance, some would choose to commune with the tomatoes for a certain number of hours. Everyone took shifts, so it felt like music was being constantly infused into the roots, the soil, and the vegetables. The plant was being held in the vibration of Love in whatever unique way that person had to offer.

People had short time slots, so work was never a burden. Everyone was provided for; money was unnecessary. There was enough for all to share. Anybody could come and tend the vegetables, pick, distribute, or cook them. Everyone had a job, from planting the seeds to harvesting the crops. It was a completely harmonious operation independent of all the other departments of the city but part of the greater whole. Within the gardening community some would tend the soil and some would plant the seeds. Different shifts would pray, chant, weed, water or distribute. If we wanted to dig a hole, the soil just moved itself and created a hole. One's needs or requests were telepathically sent, and the soil responded. Everything worked like that. We had many fruit trees. We sang to them, played crystal bowls to them, danced around them, wove light around them and communicated with them telepathically. We told them how beautiful they were and how much we appreciated the offerings they gave us. There was no disease.

The fruit was all perfect, and so we just gathered it up and shared it with the people.

Garden beds had many different shapes—rectangular, square, all geometric shapes. They were designed that way on purpose. Each shape we used, such as diamond, hexagon, octagon or circle, was part of a grand design, fitting into a greater whole. We used the same geometric design as the grids which ran through the city, the fields, and the water. They kept everything vibrant and alive, so hard physical work was not needed. Everything was so vital and full of light that when someone needed to work with the soil, it would just co-operate—the many light particles in the soil made it easy to work together.

There was no payment or currency. No money was needed; we were all so overjoyed to be of service that we would say, "Oh, may I do that?" We felt privileged to be of service. We spent time in the fields if that was our chosen work. We would go into meditation and connect telepathically to all living things. We would hold the vision of everything in perfection.

CHAPTER 13
HEALING

Healing was a part of the training that everyone received. It was passed down from person to person. The children were all taught that they had healing abilities as a normal part of life. They were taught how to bring down the golden light, focus it through their hands, and work with it. Students were given many tools to use as well. They learned how to use their intuition and insight, as well as how to use light as a laser beam for medical procedures and surgeries. The light was held in great reverence, and people were taught never to abuse it but to only use it for good.

Shape-shifting

They were able to shape-shift, especially in the earlier Lemurian times when their bodies were subtler. Shape-shifting had to do with levels of consciousness and adaptation and could be used for many purposes: traveling, dreaming, moving between dimensions, etc. It was all one and the same. Shape-shifting was used to remind people who they were, especially as people got older and denser. Healers would visit clients in their dreams to assist their healing. They could enter the dreams of people who were forgetting their true nature as angels or as forgotten beloved ones known to them, such as their mothers. In the dream, the healer would help that person to restore the heart, to remember Love, and to know that they were Love.

People only became sick because they forgot that they were Love and loved. This was after The Fall when we had moved out of Wholeness. Before The Fall, there was no sickness as such, and healing was only needed to keep people in balance. After The Fall, there were tumors and disease. Some of the healers remembered their craft and taught others.

Tools for Healing

Crystals

Healers had many tools at their disposal, and all healers had their own special crystal. They were taught all the properties of stones and crystals, which ones to use for disease and which to use for light activations. Crystals were considered sacred because they had special powers that could be activated; however, they could only work in conjunction with the consciousness of the healer and had no power in and of themselves.

Telepathy, Medical Intuition, Sound

Telepathy was used to share knowledge and skills with others on the team. This telepathic communication was used to help direct a client focus on a particular area of concern/need or to send a vision of what it should look like in Wholeness. Some healers were skilled with diagnosing the location of the problem just like medical intuitives do today while others used their gifts to restore the problem area to Wholeness.

Some healers were adept at using sound: toning, chanting, crystal bowls, Tibetan bowls, chimes, or singing.

Tool Kit

All healers were given a basic tool kit and taught how to use their innate abilities. They also had direct contact with their guides and helpers on the higher planes and just asked for what they needed from them. Healing was taught as a very natural and normal part of life. Some healers were better than others and would be trained to develop their abilities further and to specialize in certain aspects. More advanced students were taught to include the dolphins in their work, using the language of light in the DNA. They were trained to use the energy of their golden cord to connect telepathically with the dolphins in order to bring knowledge, wisdom, Love, and joy to assist with the healing.

Healing Temples

There were special healing temples for individuals, plants, and/or animals with different geometrically shaped chambers—like pyramids or spheres, for example—that enhanced the healing process. In addition, there were many different shapes set into the walls, such as pentagons, hexagons, octagons, or triangles. Energies of Love and Wholeness flowed from the grids of the Great Temple out into the whole city and all the healing temples. It was constantly being charged and re-charged. This energy pulsed from the walls and floors of every chamber.

Diverse teams of healers worked in the healing temples. All had extensive training in all the different healing modalities, such as light, sound, crystal bowls, voice, touch, toning, and crystals. If there was a new download of information or healing energies, the healers would receive it into their energy fields from the grid and then transmit it to anyone who needed to receive it.

Some healers used grids of different colored crystals that would send beams of colored light into the patient. Others would lay crystals on and around the individual needing healing, and the team would form a circle and send light through their hands to activate the crystals. Depending on the issue, the healers might or might not touch the person's body; instead, they might work in the auric/etheric field.

Healers worked with all forms of energy by holding the vision of everything in perfection. They saw the individual already healed, whole, and perfect. Firstly, the blueprint was downloaded from the archives of the whole, healed being. Then the team would hold the intention of restoring that being to its original Wholeness in alignment with the blueprint. The healers would hold the vision of this perfection, then sing, tone, visualize, or any combination of these modalities. They were taught in their training to be able to diagnose what was out of alignment and/or somehow contaminated.

People got out of alignment, especially if they traveled out of the city or off-planet, visiting places of a lower frequency. When they needed help restoring their Wholeness blueprint, they would go to the alignment healing chamber. To get there, they would step through the entrance which was an arbor filled with beautiful flowers.

Once in the chamber, the person would step through pillars of colored light created by the sunlight coming through the crystals in the walls or roof. He or she would draw from each color what was needed and by the end would be in perfect balance. If more was needed, healers would hold the vision of Wholeness and sing or tone the individual back to Wholeness. One way to do that was to sing the people's names which held their perfect blueprint of Beingness. Some tribes still practice this form of healing to bring a person back in alignment with their True Nature.

CHAPTER 14
CONNECTIONS WITH OTHER CIVILIZATIONS

As Lemurians, we had very advanced technology compared to other civilizations on Earth that we wanted to share to help others. We developed technologies specifically to help more primitive civilizations that were also on earth at this time. Arrangements would be made in council for teams of people with specialized knowledge of healing or technology to come forward. The Council would discuss what information would be shared and then arrangements would be made to travel using telepathy. There was no limitation on travel, we just saw ourselves where we wanted to be and projected ourselves there. We felt that it was part of our higher purpose for our technology to be taken elsewhere to be of service. We saw it as an extension of our service, similar to what is happening now where some people are vibrating with the resonance of the Healed Earth and some are still functioning at the frequency of the Old Earth. Those with the codes for the Healed Earth activated are assisting others to move to the new frequency.

The Lemurians vibrated at the frequency of perfection while other human groups on earth were very primitive and animalistic; they were the ones who evolved from apes. Lemurians had the connection to Source that the humans didn't. We saw that the cave people were striving to evolve and that they were simple and like children.

Our civilization was much more advanced, and because of our compassion and our desire to serve, we came in our pods and appeared to the cave people like angels.

In the beginning we would appear to them in spirit form but as we became accustomed to being in the lower density, we appeared as people more like them that they could understand and relate to.

We also had interaction with beings from the star systems; Sirius, Venus, Orion, Andromeda, Arcturus, the Pleiades and Alpha Centuri. We visited each other and shared our technologies, skills, the logistics of incorporating Wholeness as an underlying matrix, and how to keep everything we built or created connected to that matrix. We showed the others how the energy of the original matrix of Wholeness flowed through everything that was created, performed or spoken in order to maintain a balanced and complete organization.

We brought this information with us when we came to earth from the stars, and we developed it into an intricate system of maintaining balance within a living system of buildings, people, plants and animals. As Lemurians we had the ability to shape shift very easily, so if we needed to make a long journey over difficult terrain we could take the form of a bird. If we wanted to cross oceans or travel in and out of the crystal cities on the ocean, we could take the form of dolphins. We simply focused our intention on whatever shape we wanted to assume and would shape shift into that form. We could also shape shift to travel between dimensions to connect with the temples on the etheric planes. We might fly to the Great Solar Temple in the sun in the form of an eagle or visit our spirit helpers in any form we chose.

Earth was sourced by all of the different star systems. Beings from these star systems were often on planet assisting us.

Each one had its own flavor of technological advancement, so there was much exchange of information with civilizations that were very advanced. Some beings went back to their star systems after sharing their technology while others stayed to monitor and refine it.

We shared designs that were part of universal knowledge with our interplanetary brothers. We were part of an intergalactic brotherhood that shared knowledge. It is only in the last 2000 years that this knowledge has not been available. We have been sourced from the very beginning with information coming in from our galactic brothers.

Andromeda

From Andromeda we received information on healing and technology. They had the machinery that was able to reconstitute a body from a single cell of a body. For anything that was going on emotionally, there were machines that automatically read where the person was off balance. Then the machines would emit a frequency, sound, or color to restore balance. It is hard to describe how powerful this made a person. We learned that when someone was in complete alignment, that individual was Christed with all the power of the Christed Self. People used that technology in all walks of existence. Andromedans brought and still bring this technology on their star ships to share for healing.

Arcturia

From our work with the Arcturians, we learned that they were connected to the Elohim and were the builders' part of a team with the Pleaideans that created this planet and the whole solar system. They worked with the Elohim to create the etheric form and then with the Pleaideans to create the structure.

Sirius

We learned that the beings from Sirius had a deep understanding of working with energy of a specific frequency, the bluish/silver/white light energy of the Flame of Christ Consciousness. They showed us how they created and sent out light frequencies for healing and enlightenment. Today some of these light frequencies are being put into the crop circles that are over aquifers and are changing the frequency of our planet. The Syrians' specialty is tweaking the universe to restore harmony when other disharmonious factions upset the balance.

Venus

The Venusians shared their deep understanding of the energy of the heart and showed us how to connect through the heart. They shared the understanding of the bonding quality of Love with everything and said that it is the glue that holds all creation together. The soft pink/lavender energy which holds the frequency of Love and compassion is the energy of Divine Mother, pure Love. It sourced everything on the planet.

When materialism started to creep in, it was like a virus that ultimately killed the Venus/Goddess energy which is why we now have a patriarchal society. In contrast, before The Fall, the Lemurians communicated with beings on Venus and received a continual sourcing of Buddha/Love flow energy that anyone could tap into to create whatever was desired at any point in time. The energy was constant, like a river of life that all had flowing within them. This meant that we never had any lack or need for anything because everything was there for us. We could always have what we wanted because we had that Love energy in endless supply and could manifest it into anything we chose. We communicated telepathically with the Venusians whose planes were much less dense than here.

Pleiades

The Pleiadeans received us as the big brothers, fathers, mothers and sisters they were to us. They helped us to create this beautiful garden. We are their children. They love us so much; it's as if there is all this energy just waiting to burst onto the planet and change everything. When that happens there will be a complete transformation of the Earth. They are waiting for the time to be right. There is such a momentum gathering right now; therefore, when that time comes, we will have everything we need. The Pleiadeans are like our cheerleaders, just waiting to assist. We have all the gifts we need to make our planet as beautiful as theirs. On the Pleiades there is so much more of what is good, a purity of intent. They live in peace; hence, there is more clarity and harmony unlike here where we live in conflict. Now enough of us are ready, so the Pleiadeans can come in to help us.

Primitive Societies

In Lemurian times there were many places on the planet that had more primitive societies, communities, and cultures, and the two were coming together. It was almost as if the Lemurians were from the future living there, and the others were not in that paradigm. The native people were living by the sweat of their brows, and the Lemurians brought them Love, healing, culture, and demonstrations of harmony, peace and co-operation. We gave the cave people the idea to imitate peace and to create their own technologies for farming in their primitive way. We would study them and assess their level of intelligence and give information to the degree that they could understand it.

Water was the wire that we used for transmissions to the satellite communities. There were times when a community was ready to handle a little bit more. We would go to them, dressed in the clothes of the time. As emissaries of Light, we would give to them instead of taking from them. Generally, we used water to convey the energy, but when they were ready for a quantum leap, teachers would go among them in person.

Easter Island

For example, we traveled to the primitive societies because the native people at that time were warriors, such as those on Easter Island. The giant Moa statues are a result of this interaction. In order to shift their focus from conflict to cooperation, we gave a few demonstrations of power, calling upon the gods in prayers and ceremony. We attributed it all to the gods rather than to us, and it worked.

Our message, "Let's get together and honor these Gods," was to demonstrate that this power could be available to them if they were to build effigies to the Gods. This model of working together for honor of something higher was a ruse to get them away from focusing on pain and suffering as they had been doing for so long. The project was to take their minds off the wars that had been going on for so long.

In our demonstrations to these simple people, we showed them that we were just like them, except that our power came from this connection to the Gods. We got the people to stop fighting and to work together building the huge statues. As Lemurian teachers, we already knew how to levitate the stones, but we pretended it was the Gods moving them. The quarrying of the stones was done with tools, and once the stone was out and excavated, the Lemurian emissaries taught them how to move the giant statues using levitation.

Egypt's Pyramids

The pyramids were created in the same way. There were priests who had the consciousness of the earth and "grew" their homes—nothing was angular; everything was soft. One way to create a home was to form a shell from the earth. They were simple dwellings like hobbit houses, organic and capable of growing a garden on the roof.

Sharing the Technology of Healing

Lemurians gave their energy like a seed to people who were already on the earth. As beings of light they offered their technology to more primitive humans who were already on earth showing them their potential to be Divine Godlike Beings. They had the innate ability to hold this energy, and we taught them how to use it. We showed them how to use crystals, to find the place where physical laws melt and morph into something else and where the three dimensional world dissolves into other dimensions, multidimensional experiences, other worlds. We were able to go into this place and literally make the stones lighter than air, defying the laws of gravity. By focusing the consciousness of these other dimensions onto the stone we took energy from the crystal portal places and made it move through the air. We gave this to the more primitive societies and helped them to focus their consciousness onto the stones. We created an energy field around the stone, which literally lifted it into another dimension by directing the energy of the portals onto the stones. Then we were able to transport it where we wanted it to go. We don't have any reference points for this technology now. Sometimes groups, rather than individuals, were needed to focus in unity, to generate enough power to move the stones.

We brought the template from the mind of God down and offered it to the stone, and through our consciousness as Lemurian Masters the stone was placed in the energy of the crystal portal where physical laws were changed and anything could happen. We were able to take the energy and all the bizarre things that happened in the crystal portal and transmute them through our consciousness into physical things that to our minds now seem impossible.

Physical laws no longer applied when we focused our energy because we came from a place where anything was possible. We still have this knowledge in our DNA codes, and by activating it we will build the new world.

CHAPTER 15
DOLPHINS

Dolphins have never forgotten who they are. They live in joy and hold the keys for Wholeness for everyone who can hear them. We can connect with them by toning, visualization, or swimming with them. Dolphins still have the codes for Wholeness because they never lost the connection to Source. They transmit the codes to us encoded in their sounds and energy. Being in the water with them and receiving their transmission permeates our energy body and helps us to remember who we are. The codes are transmitted in the language of Light, which we then have to decode in our own way to bring the Light into the world. Connecting with the dolphins touches our hearts and souls and helps us to remember joy and Wholeness. When the codes come down from Source as the language of Light, the dolphins come spinning with them, spiraling down to help bring the codes in.

In Lemuria we could be dolphins or people. Moving at will, we chose whichever form we wished. We had the same consciousness and lived in joy and Wholeness. The dolphins came with us from Sirius where we all worked together in the Temple of the Eternal Flame, the Flame of the Cosmic Christ. This is the energy that is lifting the Earth into her new form at this time. We all decided to come to earth together in our light pods, using a merkabah (light body) as a light ship.

The dolphins chose to come with us to take form in a physical body. They came to help us to keep our connection to Source and remember who we are. When we sank deeper into density, we lost our connection to Source. The dolphins never did, so they agreed to come with us to "shepherd us" and help us if we got lost and went astray. They would hold the blueprint for Wholeness for us in the event we forgot who we were.

Matrix of Wholeness

That is exactly what happened. We lost our way and the dolphins have been holding the matrix of our Wholeness for us. They are now connecting with us individually and as a race, helping us to remember our Divinity. Each of us has our own pod/family that traveled with us from Sirius; connecting with that pod helps to activate the blueprint for our Wholeness. We can do this by hearing the dolphins' sounds, swimming with them, or connecting with them on the astral plane through visualization.

Dolphins have a very deep understanding of how to move in a light and organic way among all levels of Wholeness. They have a concept of the Wholeness grids and remind us how to keep connecting with them. The dolphins' moving between the grid layers keeps them in joyful fluidity. Dolphins facilitate and show us how to organically connect from individuation to Wholeness and back. They hold the high frequency blue/white energy of Sirius to assist us to move into Christ Consciousness.

Dolphins teach us how to connect lightly with joy and Love. They are both transmitters and receivers for the frequencies from Sirius and put these energies into the water just by being in it. Having the dolphins in our oceans changes the water. As the frequency moves to higher and higher levels, more is happening within a certain period of time—as though time is speeding up.

At first when we were more like spheres of light, we communicated through the light body and aura. We brought beauty into being through the combination of the mind and intention. This beauty is still held in the brains of the dolphins, who are here to help us remember the beauty and move through pain and suffering into joy.

Galactic Brain

The dolphins helped us create a galactic brain with the energies of healing wired into that brain. If our skulls were transparent, we would see lines and pulses of light, like a crystal city inside our heads. When we began to move into more defined bodies, our galactic brain assisted our creative activity by utilizing an electrical current and manifesting what we needed from the ethers. The codes for this dormant part of the brain are still held in our DNA and are activated by dolphin sounds.

As our DNA strands are reconnected, we will have access to parts of the brain that have been dormant. The dolphins spiral up through the DNA, carrying the disconnected strands and reconnecting them. Their sounds assist the process, opening the codes in our DNA. We only have to request them to do this for us, and it is done.

The whole dolphin brain pulses with colors: indigo, aqua, sapphire, magenta, pink, violet and turquoise. It is full of light that contains all the dimensions, but the dolphins don't separate dimensions. To them, there is all one great harmonious vibration, a song, a dance of life. With this dolphin brain, we create as we move. We cast images from our brain; as the images birth, they become whatever form we choose to wrap around them. All chambers of the brain are firing at 100% all the time, a huge harmonious experience. The galactic brain is like a gleaming, pulsing city of light. We can ask the dolphins to bring this galactic brain into ours and to merge with it. This is one of the activations, which Charmian does in her sessions. Their gift to us contains pulses of light like meridians or acupuncture points that fire/re-awaken all the codes.

Energy comes down from Source in spiraling galaxies around the body bringing the galactic frequency into the brain. The creative techniques we used with this brain were colors, sounds, and patterns. We need to start doing this now in our groups. The galactic pulsation is what we were in the beginning, and the dolphins still are. They are holding the energy for us here on the planet so that we can be reactivated. Now we are returning to who we are; powerful galactic energetic entities who created physical bodies around that energy. This power created everything, including our own physicality to clothe it. That was the intention when we came to live on this planet. This is why the dolphins are connecting with us now, inviting us to swim with them or to listen to their song with the intention of recovering our galactic consciousness.

CHAPTER 16
WHALES

We are now at a point in time on this planet where many are disconnected from the energy of Love. Some high beings here are connected to that energy, but it is not the same as it used to be. Now there are little tiny points of light here and there, but not like it was in Lemuria. The whales are the holders of that energy and are beaming it onto the planet for us to tune into. If we accept it, we can ask for it to be a source of Wholeness for us in our life. The whales like the dolphins are emitting the frequencies of Venus in a constant beam of the energy that we can access by tuning into the frequency of the whales telepathically. It's not as if it is coming from another planet because the whales are already here on Earth. All the water has that frequency in it, and we can ask for the Love to be brought forth from the water even as we drink it. We can ask for the blessing of Venus energy to come and open up our hearts in conjunction with the whales. Then we, too, can be the endless Love that they are.

Protectors of the Earth

Whales hold another key that is different from the dolphins: a different language. The whales hold the keys for the earth, the physical realm; the dolphins hold the keys of Light. Whales are the stewards of the earth; they have mastered the earth plane as the dolphins have mastered the astral plane. Whales have developed enormous bodies to help them to ground the vast frequency of Love, which they embody. The whales are here to protect the earth.

Through their singing and their size, they teach us to love and honor Mother Earth. Humans came to earth with the dolphins, but the whales have a different purpose. People have become disconnected from Gaia, our Earth Mother, and have forgotten to honor and thank her. The whales are holding the space of Love for Mother Earth for us until we find our way back to Love. They are teaching us how to stay grounded and how to stay in Love. It all works as a delicate inner weaving.

The whales have the memory of all the templates of the different planets and star systems and the moments before separation, so they hold the original blueprints of Wholeness. They are constantly transmitting these blueprints. As we begin to remember, we are able to receive the blueprints that bring us back to Wholeness. The whales will stay on Earth until enough of us have received the blueprints and are able to hold the frequency again for ourselves. The whales also have access to all the archives, containing the blueprints of Wholeness for all civilizations in many galaxies and universes.

Seeing whales helps those who are not of a higher consciousness to feel awe at their magnificence. For instance, people who are not in touch with themselves or are caught up in their minds and their beliefs, are reminded when they see whales that there is something greater out there. Few people ever get to see anything so big or to see one of God's creations that is so Godlike. The sight of a whale breaching or hearing their song takes people into awe, and they take that memory home with them to help them to remember God.

Holders of Love

While the dolphins brought the energy from the Great Central Sun down to the earth through Sirius and the Christ flame, the whales brought that energy in through Venus's Temple of Love. Both are embodying Love as they fill the waters with Love through their songs and their presence. Their message is simple: "Remember Love. Remember that you are Love, and remember that you are loved."

Whales hold us all in Love. It's like being in a big, warm bath. It doesn't matter what we have done or where we have been. They just totally hold us in Love. They demonstrate for us how to be in Love in a physical body. They hold that energy for all of us and are very patient. Whales have been holding the Love vibration and waiting, holding Love like a garland of roses in the waters all around the earth. These beautiful giants are in all Earth's oceans, constantly renewing Love and saying, "Just come and receive it. When it all gets too hard and too much, just come and receive Love."

Helping the Whales

We need to remember the language of the whales; we used to talk to them or sing to them, and they would sing back. We all knew the song of Love then, but humans forgot the song. The whales continued singing, and now they are singing us back because we are remembering the song. Soon we will be able to sing together again. If you remember the song, please go to the ocean (either physically or ethereally) and join them in singing the Song of Wholeness.

The whales need our help at this time. They are such vast, gentle beings and are asking us to stop killing them. Sonar testing by the military is very painful for them. They can't protect themselves from us, so they ask us that we raise our consciousness in order to raise the consciousness of others and help us to save the whales in places like Alaska and Japan where they are still hunted or trapped. Whales need to be respected and honored as elders/wise ones, and they need to be free.

We can help them by giving them more attention and focusing on reconnecting to our Divine Essence and embodying it. We are currently not taking this issue seriously enough, so they are asking us to focus on creating more space to bring the frequency of our Divine Selves into our bodies. We can connect with the whales visually or through sound. We need to come together in our groups because memories are anchored in our DNA, and each person has a piece of the whole. With their help, we can recreate the grids filled with Love and Wholeness for all.

CHAPTER 17
THE FALL

Lemuria had two distinct time periods, before and after The Fall. In the beginning we were constantly connected to the Source by the grids that ran through every part of our cities. We were fed and renewed by that constant connection, so there was never any sense of separation or isolation. In time, we forgot the connection, and that time is known as The Fall. As we descended into deeper and deeper levels of disconnection, we moved further away from Source. Our energy fields became more and more dense like a layer of padding and numbness. We didn't understand as things began to change, and we forgot who we were. We moved away from remembering that we were Love and could create our own resources from within.

Being of Service and Sharing Light and Knowledge

How did this happen? There was an evolutionary pull from another plane—temptation disguised as service We had certain stations in our city where we stood in a circle in our pods and activated beams of light by our intention and sound to teleport ourselves to materialize in the new place. We knew that other civilizations needed the Light and help; we had so much knowledge that we wanted to share it with them. Our lifestyle was so harmonious that we wanted other civilizations to achieve the same level of balance and harmony.

In the beginning it was fine; we were able to keep the grids energized because we still had the connection to Source and the other star systems. The cities and gardens were so beautiful; there were pools and flowers and trees, unicorns and dolphins to play with. We still lived in Wholeness, wonder, and joy. We had fruit and vegetables and trees, and we loved our world. It was physical paradise without pain. We were the innocents in the Garden of Eden.

Forgetting Who We Were

As we descended further into density, we began to lose our connections with the star systems. We began to have more cultural exchanges with the Atlanteans at first. Then Atlantis began to degenerate into materialism with its concepts of separation between "Us" and "Them" and division between "elites" and "inferiors." An example of this was the Atlanteans used the cave people to interbreed with animals to make a lower class of slave people to work for them.

Unfortunately, some of these concepts of materialism gained a foothold in Lemuria and spread like a wild fire. The Atlanteans created the situation that people who were in touch with the star people were "Us," and everyone else was "Them." The star people refused to participate in that, so they withdrew from consciously interacting any longer.

We hadn't realized how much living in the dense vibrations of other civilizations would affect us. We began to forget we were Light and became too involved in their dense frequencies. This opened the door for lower frequency extra-terrestrials to come in and exploit Earth and her inhabitants.

Then we were lost. We had no roots or connection to our star homes. This was the beginning of The Fall. Once it set in, the cancer spread. We were on our own. The distortion was love of power, which translated into accumulated wealth. The Atlanteans always wanted more, which looked to others like materialism. "I have this power and these things, and you don't" seemed to be their philosophy and the way they lived. The off-planet nations were unwilling to give us any more assistance because they felt we were using their gifts in an improper way.

While all this was happening, more Lemurians left Lemuria to go around the Earth to help the others return home, but then they, too, got stuck. Soon the grids had no one to sustain or renew them so the cities began to disintegrate. At one time, the buildings' consciousness was intertwined with the people who created them and worked within them, but that was gone. Without that interaction, they couldn't maintain their structure so the cities lost their strength and dissipated. The continent of Lemuria sank beneath the ocean. It was like the time in Montsegur in the Midi-Pyrenees of southwestern France. When the Cathars knew the end had come, they walked joyously into the fire. As Lemurians, we went back to the water and Light from which we had come.

Other than being of service and sharing our knowledge with other civilizations, why would we have chosen to experience such separation? As Lemurians, we were confident that we could hold the high energies anywhere, so we chose to see how far into density could we travel and hold the Light uncontaminated. The mission was to bring the Light to the lowest plane of density. The question was whether we could maintain the integrity and Wholeness of the Light within us when we descended that far into the density.

When Lemuria sank, we were interacting with primitive people. Some of us became emissaries who were still able to maintain contact telepathically with extra-terrestrial civilizations, but gradually their numbers reduced to just a few people. Some of the Native American tribes had and still have contact with the star people because they didn't adopt technology so they remained in contact with the land and primitive ways.

Returning to Our Essence

The memory of The Fall is imprinted in our cellular memory. There are two images. One is that we are going back to Oneness, to Wholeness while the other is "What happened? What went wrong? How did we fail?" In the end, we abandoned our physical existence and returned to the place of pure essence. We returned to innocence. We need to clear the memory of not succeeding so we can maintain that state of original innocence in the negativity of the third dimension.

We can connect with each other in our Light bodies as we did in the Lemurian temples because we are beings of Light. We are bringing free, clear, unchained, and unbound Light essence into our physical bodies as they are now. It doesn't matter what state others are in around us when we can be the Light. We don't have to make others any different. If they don't choose to be in the Light, it doesn't affect where we are because we are in the Light that helps us to be in the world but not of it.

We can be unattached to outcomes or experiences because we know who we are. Our temple teams are still spheres of color in our light bodies. We can draw on those colors and energies anytime, any place we are.

When the earth shifts, all our levels and existences will be brought together into Wholeness. We are not there yet, so as a race we need to reconnect with our teams to help each other to hold the frequency of Love. We need to do this now.

Before The Fall, before "Us" and "Them" consciousness came from Atlantis, there was a harmony and a holistic quality in everything that existed. We looked at how each creation was going to affect every aspect of our being. Everything was designed with that paradigm in mind. If it wasn't something that was going to benefit every aspect of our beingness, then it wasn't created. This element was lost when things started to change into "Us" and "Them;" it was left out of the equation.

This is when things got out of balance. Earth felt it, shifted, and everything came apart. It was a cleansing similar to what we are having now. Mother Earth can only take so much, and then she says, "Ok, enough."

CHAPTER 18
THE RETURN

Those of us who were in Lemuria are the oldest souls on the planet, the original seedlings. We have come back for the return to Oneness for ourselves and Earth. We carry within our DNA the templates for the Lemurian light codes that will activate the earth grids and create the blueprint of Wholeness for Earth and all its inhabitants. The blueprint comes down as a matrix. There are others who have the codes but not those from Lemuria, and they have their roles, too. When these Light codes are activated, we will be able to shift our frequencies into the fifth dimensional lightbody and lift ourselves and Earth into Oneness again.

Reawakening

Some of us are beginning to remember who we are and why we are here. We are recognizing the need to raise our vibrations to remember how to open, sustain, and share the blueprint of Wholeness. In order to do this, we must eat high vibrational foods and monitor our thoughts. We must keep our bodies and minds clean to hold these high vibrations. In addition, those who are remembering who they are need to share their memories by making them audible or visible to others. We have been afraid to share our knowledge because historically we have been ridiculed, persecuted, or excluded for being "different" than the mainstream.

As Earth's vibration increases, the ancient temples and the crystal cities that withdrew into the higher dimensions to keep their energies intact when darkness was coming are now being reactivated. The time for reawakening is now. The Lemurian temple teams are finding each other. Each member of the team holds a key aspect that will activate when all the pieces come together.

As before, Lemurian gridmasters are receiving the codes and translating them so that they can be received on the Earth plane. Waves of sound and light are carrying the new Light codes. Since crystals are able to transmit energy, those places on Earth where there are many crystals in the land are natural conductors and amplifiers of energy in the global grids. The vibration for the New Earth is already here. This is the completion of all our incarnations on the earth plane. We are here to ground the energy of the Lords of Light, the Elohim, into physicality. We must remember that we hold the blueprint. As we open it up for ourselves, we open it for all. We must see it in each one and know that this is the truth and reality of who we are.

To do this, we are seeking out others who hold a specific resonating DNA so that we can co-create on a conscious level with those families and groups. We are gathering in our temple circles again, but many of us are not yet aware that is what is occurring. We only know we are being drawn to one another in spiritual groups where we are remembering our spirits and starting to remember who we are. This is a revival of the ancient circles in the temples.

Helping Mother Earth Return to Wholeness

We can do much to assist Mother Earth at this time. The moment we walk upon the earth, we impregnate it with our consciousness; therefore, those of us who have the conscious knowledge of the codes of Oneness radiate that to others. Since Earth has lost the memory of the original Oneness grid, we are reminding her that this vibration has once more become manifest.

As we receive the new light codes and walk them into the Earth grids, a new note has been added to the symphony that is traveling around the Earth in the crystal grids. Many are receiving the missing note. As it resonates in them, it is helping to restore the balance of the Earth. Some receive the note as sound that can then be transmitted in singing or toning. Others receive it as symbols, patterns of light that can be transmitted through art or visualization. We are reconnecting with our Lemurian teams who came with us from the stars. We need to know that we each carry the others inside us and are always directly connected to the group heart.

We have come to a place where we have lost the words that connect us to the inner core so the consciousness of Oneness is struggling to come through. In order to return to the joyous, multi-faceted way of living and being, we need to feel the greater "I" in our hearts. Our heart is really the hub where everything connects. Every train of thought and every fiber of feeling is connected to the heart. The more we realize this, the more the energy can flow from our hearts into every aspect of our life to nurture and increase the vibration of Mother Earth.

Another way we can help Mother Earth is to remind each other of our Oneness as we are all connected and have an intricate role to play. Everyone has a gift to give. All can work in harmony and add their pieces to the whole. We can create Love, be Love, and be Wholeness. We can be creators. We can be balance, a conscious co-creation with male and female energy. We can give our gifts and remember our purpose. We can help one another, care for one another, and focus on the good of the greater whole. This is already happening. A segment of more evolved beings are recognizing the necessity of connectedness, balance, and love, and are helping each other. This awareness is growing.

Visualization is another approach to helping Mother Earth at this time. In Lemuria, we did our healing work by holding the vision of the person already healed, in Wholeness, and connected with that blueprint. We can do this now for Mother Earth, holding the vision of her healed and transformed into Wholeness.

Coming Full Circle

Originally, we chose to enter Earth's density to bring light into the darkness. Our consciousness is different now because we have the power of the dark and the light. We have no fear of the dark because this new frequency of light was born from the void, and it contains all the power of darkness and light. This is the new consciousness of the awakening ones who are choosing to complete the cycle of transformation at this time. Now it's time to create a new form of Light that can be in density and yet hold the frequency and the pure Love of Oneness.

We have come full circle from the Golden Light of Oneness through the darkness into the new form of the Cosmic Christ. The blue flame in every strand of DNA is enabling the human race to mutate into a galactic vehicle for the embodiment of Christ Consciousness. This was the purpose of The Fall—to experience the Darkness and maintain our Light. We are the ones who are fulfilling the Divine Purpose of awakening the blueprint of Wholeness for the embodiment of our Divinity as we create the golden dawn on the New Earth.

It is time for us to claim our Divinity, be open to receive it, and agree to embody it. In doing so, we set our souls free. The chains that were holding us in separation are melting; our wings are opening as we embody the energy of the Cosmic Christ more and more. We must invite the cells of our hearts to be transmuted in the Blue Flame of the Living Christ. We must claim our birthright now on behalf of awakening humanity. We see hearts aflame. We decree it is so and see all forms of separation being transmuted now into the Flame of the Cosmic Christ.

From full consciousness through total forgetfulness and seeming isolation, we are moving back to the ancient experience of circular living. The pendulum is swinging back to its center again. As we swing back, we realize that we are not alone and that all of our experiences which caused us so much stress in the isolation from our core are just illusions. We had to fill them with our sense of reality in order to understand them. Now we are returning and bringing a wealth of information from Source, from which it came.

Lemurian and Other Lightworkers

Because the dolphins and whales know and hold the frequency of Oneness, they are a source of remembrance for those who are returning. It is more difficult now because we have been living in the lower vibrations of the third dimension and have not had the support of the whole society. Thus it is more important than ever for Lemurian and other Lightworkers to find each other, remember their Light, and bring in the vibration of Wholeness through toning, visualization, dance, and music—anything that opens the heart in as many ways as possible and helps the Lightworkers support one another. In addition, they could live together in co-operative communities and bring the energies of loving oneness into other communities who could benefit. Then they could return to their own communities for support and the reminder that they are the Light. This form of evolution as civilization is growing and helping individuals remember who they are.

When the Lemurian civilizations became denser, they were shocked and surprised because they didn't know how to get back. Now we are aware of our evolutionary path and abilities. We are aware that we have lived in density for eons and have developed our Light. Lemurian and other Lightworkers are increasing in numbers and strength; we are remembering that we can be in this dense world as a community. As we remember who we are, we can help others evolve and thereby continue to evolve in our own strength and purpose. All are evolving towards the Light in their own ways, but the Lightworkers have healing gifts and the ability to assist others to raise their vibrations. If we can help others raise their vibration by even one iota, then we have done our work on the planet.

Following the Inner Call

Basically, we all live as One and that means that on some level, each one of us knows what everyone else is making, thinking, and creating. That goes for all of creation, so now many of us are being drawn back to connecting with nature again. We are hearing our brothers and sisters in the mountain spirits, tree spirits, and ocean spirits. With these co-beings, we are nurturing that Oneness. The more we experience the joy, bliss, and creativity, the more we are energized by this return flow—much like migrating birds. Many of us are now following this inner call.

We are being drawn to different parts of our planet where effective co-creative groups are already expecting us. We feel "called" and find others who were "called" there also. By nature, we are mobile people. We fare best when we don't hold onto one person, place, or particular activity exclusively. We need to realize that while we are still in linear time and move through things one after the other, such as one area of the planet, one activity, relationship, or experience, eventually we will not be so time-bound. In our consciousness, we will be able to see that it is all happening together, and the bliss will increase when we know that we are together and not separated by linear time.

We are becoming more aware of the many levels of bliss that are happening simultaneously as we are finding our partners of old and coming together in sacred union sharing our energies and returning to bliss and orgasmic joy. We are aware of the many beings—dolphins, whales, stars, trees, elementals—who are joining us in our ecstasy. We are learning not to exclude anyone anymore. We are beginning to forget to say, "I can't" and remembering to say, "Yes I can".

Every thought we think, every image we see, every possibility we can imagine becomes one joyous vibration pervading and uniting everything at the same time. We realize that All is One. All is here as One.

Lemurian Grid Masters Ushering Cycles In and Out

We are the Lemurian Masters who incarnate at the beginning and end of the great cycles of civilization on the Earth. We come to assist with the transition from one level of consciousness to the next and hold the codes for each new frequency being seeded onto the planet. Twin Flames come together during these lifetimes to work in partnership to anchor the energies for each new phase of human evolution. We hold the memories of the Beauty at the beginning of each cycle and the grief from the destruction at the end of each cycle. Many of us are held back from being with our Twin Flames in this lifetime because we have unresolved grief from losing them in the destruction of Atlantis and Lemuria. We must clear this grief because we are meant to work with our polarity partners at this time to assist mother Earth in her return to Oneness.

Physical and Emotional Challenges at This Time

The energies for the healed Earth are vibrating at a high frequency and rippling around the globe. As this occurs, they are causing a host of physical and emotional reactions as they enter our energy bodies. The memories of pain and abuse that we carry are resonating at a much lower frequency, so when the energy of pure Love hits our energy field, it triggers reactions as the body clears old energies.

Many people are experiencing pain in the physical, especially the bones as we literally begin to grow a new body with a much higher crystalline frequency. We are currently in the "transition" process. As those of you who have experienced or worked with childbirth know, the transition phase of a mother in labor is the most difficult. As our bones change to a new crystalline structure, many people are experiencing pain or broken bones. Also, old fears and anxieties are surfacing, being pushed out by the energy of pure Love so that they can be cleared and released. This is the time of great healing when all old wounds are opening to be healed. It is a challenging time as we travel blindly through the process of birth, not consciously knowing that nothing less than our shining God-self is birthing. The outcome will be glorious.

As the emotions and physical problems emerge, they can feel quite overwhelming, so it does help to find a good "midwife" to assist the process. Hypnotherapy, sound and/or energy healing, and bodywork help individuals to bring in the Blueprint of Wholeness and to release the memories which are holding them in separation. The emotions arise can feel very real, but they are only memories and can be cleared very quickly with help.

Some of the physical symptoms include sudden high temperatures, coughs, colds, earaches, headaches, and digestive upsets as the body reacts to the high frequencies and literally burns off old stuck energies which are holding us in density and blocking the Light. We are reclaiming the consciousness of who we are and beginning to live it now.

This Aquarian time is for us to be more creative in the mental right brain realm. As we reconnect our DNA strands, we will have more access to the creative part of the brain again.

We have the consciousness to change all that has happened to the Earth, and that is why the memories of Lemuria are coming back. We need to clear all of the memories attached to the Fall because for many of us, these memories are preventing us from connecting and manifesting from our God-self.

Out of Ego and into Oneness

It is time to move out of ego. We must manifest now for the good of the whole, the community, and the planet. We need to clear the painful memories of The Fall because we are associating the process of manifestation with the pain of The Fall, which violated our purity and our original innocence. We lost many of our DNA strands and fell into a great void—into another consciousness. Now we can consciously reclaim our innocence. Now is time for the consummation of the whole process, the combination of consciousness and innocence fusing into One.

In the womb of the Great Mother, we came into matter. The Fall was the great moment when we brought Light into this matter as a way of the creation of duality with Divine Father and Divine Mother coming together as One in the act of Creation. It is time now to step forward and claim this power and our mastery over all the dimensions. We must claim the Light as we bring the male principle back into balance with the female principle. We created our world, the flowers, the plants, and the creatures in the Temples of Creation. We have knowledge and power encoded in our DNA. It is now time to release these memories, reactivate the codes, and return Mother Earth to Paradise, the Garden of Eden.

CHAPTER 19
HAWAII AND THE PACIFIC ISLANDS

Certain places on Earth are holding memories of Ancient Lemuria, and people are being called there either to live or visit these ancient sites that hold the frequencies of the lost civilization. New Zealand, Australia, Indonesia, Japan and all of the Pacific islands have these memories stored in the stones and the land, as well as also the west coast of North and South America: California, Brazil, Chile, Mexico, and Peru. All of these places have populations of dolphins and whales who are waiting to reconnect with us and help us to wake up and remember who we are.

The Hawaiian Islands are a generating point that is connected to all the other Pacific islands. We brought the codes in here and put them into a form in which they could travel through the ley lines of the Earth grids. We translated them so that they could be received on the Earth plane. Many Lemurian masters are being called to return to Hawaii to have their dormant codes activated. Nothing is ever lost. It isn't something we need to learn, just remember. These codes can be activated by sound, by interaction with whales and dolphins in any manner, or by healers who hold the frequencies.

The Big island of Hawaii has more of the energy of Lemuria after The Fall. The pure vibrations that existed before The Fall are more accessible on Maui, Lanai, and Kauai. This is a subtler, more refined energy there so it is easier to bring in the blueprints for the Wholeness matrix. On the Big Island of Hawaii we need to translate the energies through the filters in our energy fields to refine it, but on Maui this isn't necessary, and this is why there are so many Lightworkers there.

The underlying grid is already in place to anchor the blueprint of Wholeness. It is strong, easy to access and work with.

Maui has a strong communal spirit that needs to be grounded into all of Hawaii. The Haleakala volcano there was a very powerful energy center in Lemuria. This energy makes the Lemurian frequency more easily accessible for the teachers, healers, and leaders of the New Dawn upon the Earth, who are to bring back the ancient teachings and truths. As we reconnect to Source and become whole and healed, the energy reverberates like ripples on a pond and touches many more.

When we are in the water with the cetaceans hearing their sounds or just seeing them, we can easily receive the codes that will help us remember Wholeness and Love. When enough people remember, the whole planet can return to the Lemurian consciousness of pure Love and Wholeness, but this time it will be in our dense physical bodies. When the frequency of unconditional Love is resonating in our energy fields, it will affect and activate the energies of anyone who comes into contact with us.

Ceremony to Re-open the Grid of the Crystal City in Kaelekakua Bay

On August 20, 2006, a group of us stood in a circle by the ocean and toned with the intention of reopening the grid of the crystal city, which is out in the ocean between Kealakekua Bay and Honaunau Bay, the two bays where the dolphins are most active. Then we turned to face the setting sun in a semi-circle and toned again into the energy of the sun with the intention of reconnecting with the frequency of Wholeness through the Great Central Sun.

As we did this, several people saw with their inner sight a city of light appear over the ocean on the horizon. We then formed our circle on the grass at Manini Beach and grounded the energy into the Earth grids which completed the re-activation of the temple. Since then, I have discovered crystal cities in the crater of Haleakala, Kalalau Valley on Kauai, Manele Bay on Lanai, and Huelo on Maui. I'm sure there are others waiting to be re-discovered.

Those who have reconnected with these frequencies have the energy of the New Earth already resonating in their fields. The energy shift is beginning in Hawaii, and from there it is traveling out across the Earth. The energies are transmitted and received through the great power centers of the Earth which amplify the energy and pass it on. The Lightworkers carry this frequency in their energy field once it has been activated which is why we are doing so much traveling now.

After spending five months on Hawaii receiving activations, I then found myself traveling for six months carrying the frequencies to England, especially Stonehenge and Glastonbury; then on to California; New Grange in Ireland; Salt Lake City, Utah; Sedona, Arizona; Santa Fe, New Mexico; and Mt Shasta, California. While at these places, I passed on the frequencies in my workshops to the participants who were activated and then carried them on their own travels. Just by traveling, we are walking the Light into being when we find ourselves visiting the great energy vortex centers of the planet, such as Macchu Picchu, Giza, Ayers rock in Australia, The Grand Tetons, Stonehenge, New Grange in Ireland, and/or the Mayan pyramids of the Yucatan. A friend and I found ourselves in Boynton Canyon in Sedona, Arizona, up on a ledge looking out across the valley.

There on the opposite side was a complete Lemurian city with temples and pillars that look as if they have been carved into the rock. There was a whole group of Lemurian beings waiting there for us to reactivate the temple.

Toning is especially powerful to transmit the codes as the sound is received by the rocks and the crystals at the sacred sites and by everyone who subsequently visits there. When I visit ancient sites, I always tone and then go into silence to see what message the stones have for me. Just very simple ceremony, prayers, toning or sitting in silence will help to connect with the memories of the place.

As we hold the Blueprint for the healed, transformed Earth, she is slowly moving into that energy; however, individuals are experiencing many challenges at this time, and so is Mother Earth. She is cleansing herself as is evident in the increase in earthquakes, tsunamis, and volcanic activity. She is shifting the energy of the Old Earth from her plates as we are shifting the energy of our old consciousness of separation from our bones. We are growing a new body of Light and so is Mother Earth.

It is time for all of us to wake up,
to remember Who We are,
and to Birth the New Earth.

AFTERWORD
CHARMIAN'S PURPOSE AS CHANNELED BY HER TEAM MEMBER

Charmian swims with the dolphins on a regular basis, and she was in Lemuria. She was one of the original Star Seeds that brought the codes for Lemuria here. She is passing them on to people who are ready to receive them now. The codes come through her in every part of her work; they remind people that they are whole. The journeying work that she does is a direct link to bring people back to Wholeness, back to Love. She holds that within her. She is here to remind people who they are.

It is time now to activate the light codes in the DNA that were downloaded in Lemuria. These codes will help us to activate our Divine Human-Galactic Light Body and allow us to create a new reality, which could manifest as successful relationships, financial abundance, or a beautiful home. These codes that Charmian helps us to activate also enable us to magnetize our Soul Kin to us, bringing back that feeling of community, never feeling alone again. Charmian is also is here to welcome the new children into the world through her work as a doula and hypnobabies ™ instructor.

We can now return to the way society was organized and operating in Lemuria. The ancient Lemurian connection is still here although many people don't think about it now.

The technology, the healing, the Love is what Charmian is. She is connectedness. She is Love. She remembers who she is.

She remembers her connectedness to Lemuria, the dolphins, the whales, the angels, and the guides. She is a messenger. She has come here directly to remind people who they are. Her method is working through guided imagery and hypnosis and is a gift because people love to journey back to who they are, and they don't know how to do that.

Journeying is a unique gift because it takes people to places they can't access alone and that adds to the greater whole. When her partner comes, it will be a coming together in perfect balance. She has been working with the Goddess side and the partner will bring the male side. As they come together for the good of the whole in ecstatic connection to God, they will be modeling what everyone can aspire to attain—connection to Source on a deeper, passionate, more intimate level.

Being on Maui is home to Charmian. The memories are very close to the surface here, and they are very easily accessible. She carries them all in her energy field because she was a grid master in Lemuria. The blueprints came through her for everything, and other people decoded their pieces. She held the master key, so when she goes traveling, the same thing happens; people are able to open the keys which are appropriate to them through tuning-in to her energy fields. This happens either through the groups that she teaches or individually through sound and visualization sessions. It doesn't matter what we do. She opens up her energy field through singing, drumming, toning or journeying, so people can receive whatever they need.

Charmian is a connector and joiner. She connects people to the Light; she can see where the thread is broken and can fix or heal it. She holds hands with another person and then holds the hand of Light and makes the connection for anyone she comes into contact with.

She connects them to the Light where it is broken by words, actions, or sounds; she knows the keys to unlock the connection to the Pure Light or essence of each person.

She is here to bring the codes from Lemuria to help seed the New Earth. The whole new form is already resonating in her energy field. Hawaii is the place where the new energy begins, so her energy field has already accepted and integrated the new frequencies for the New Earth. She is bringing back the Lemurian way of Love in the way that she knows how—loving and caring for everyone equally. She cares for everyone as if they were part of the whole, and everyone is special.

Wherever she travels, she is seeding the frequencies into the land and into people, and then they transmit them to others who they come into contact with. She has a strong connection to the sound part of Lemuria, and is responsible for getting people together to co-create a focus point using sound. Charmian has the capacity to ask the right questions to elicit the information needed to help them resonate in harmony with their Higher Selves, their Souls' Purposes and with their bigger pictures. One of her gifts is that she can psychically see distortions in the information that is coming in, which means that it is not in alignment with the Wholeness Matrix for that person. She has the ability to guide them back into alignment with their True Self.

ABOUT THE AUTHOR

In 1980 Charmian had a Near Death Experience in which she returned to Oneness and remembered Who She Is. Since that time she has been assisting others through her workshops and personal sessions to reconnect with their own Divine Self and to activate the DNA codes for ascension.

She has remembered her many lives as a teacher and healer in the mystery schools always guiding her students to find the God Within and to empower themselves.

Since moving to Hawaii in 2006, Charmain has brought forward many memories of Ancient Lemuria; where we live in Oneness and used our intention and connection to the Source to create everything we need in our lives. Her work now is to bring back the teams who worked in the Ancient Crystal Cities so that we can begin to create our New World.

Charmian can be reached on her website www.cominghometolemuria.com (all one word). She offers sessions by phone and in person guiding clients into their own memories of the beautiful lives in Lemuria and on many other star systems as well as incarnations on Earth.

Other Books By Ozark Mountain Publishing, Inc.

Dolores Cannon
Conversations with Nostradamus,
  Volume I, II, III
Jesus and the Essenes
They Walked with Jesus
Between Death and Life
A Soul Remembers Hiroshima
Keepers of the Garden.
The Legend of Starcrash
The Custodians
The Convoluted Universe - Book One,
  Two, Three, Four
Five Lives Remembered
The Three Waves of Volunteers and the
  New Earth
Stuart Wilson & Joanna Prentis
The Essenes - Children of the Light
Power of the Magdalene
Beyond Limitations
Atlantis and the New Consciousness
The Magdalene Version
O.T. Bonnett, M.D./Greg Satre
Reincarnation: The View from Eternity
What I Learned After Medical School
Why Healing Happens
M. Don Schorn
Elder Gods of Antiquity
Legacy of the Elder Gods
Gardens of the Elder Gods
Reincarnation...Stepping Stones of Life
Aron Abrahamsen
Holiday in Heaven
Out of the Archives – Earth Changes
Sherri Cortland
Windows of Opportunity
Raising Our Vibrations for the New Age
Michael Dennis
Morning Coffee with God
God's Many Mansions
Nikki Pattillo
Children of the Stars
A Spiritual Evolution
Rev. Grant H. Pealer
Worlds Beyond Death
A Funny Thing Happened on the Way to
  Heaven
Maiya & Geoff Gray-Cobb
Angels - The Guardians of Your Destiny
Seeds of the Soul
Sture Lönnerstrand
I Have Lived Before
Arun & Sunanda Gandhi
The Forgotten Woman
Claire Doyle Beland
Luck Doesn't Happen by Chance

James H. Kent
Past Life Memories As A Confederate
  Soldier
Dorothy Leon
Is Jehovah An E.T
Justine Alessi & M. E. McMillan
Rebirth of the Oracle
Donald L. Hicks
The Divinity Factor
Christine Ramos, RN
A Journey Into Being
Mary Letorney
Discover The Universe Within You
Debra Rayburn
Let's Get Natural With Herbs
Jodi Felice
The Enchanted Garden
Susan Mack & Natalia Krawetz
My Teachers Wear Fur Coats
Ronald Chapman
Seeing True
Rev. Keith Bender
The Despiritualized Church
Vara Humphreys
The Science of Knowledge
Karen Peebles
The Other Side of Suicide
Antoinette Lee Howard
Journey Through Fear
Julia Hanson
Awakening To Your Creation
Irene Lucas
Thirty Miracles in Thirty Days
Mandeep Khera
Why?
Robert Winterhalter
The Healing Christ
James Wawro
Ask Your Inner Voice
Tom Arbino
You Were Destined to be Together
Maureen McGill & Nola Davis
Live From the Other Side
Anita Holmes
TWIDDERS
Walter Pullen
Evolution of the Spirit
Cinnamon Crow
Teen Oracle
Chakra Zodiac Healing Oracle
Jack Churchward
Lifting the Veil on the Lost Continent of
  Mu
Guy Needler
The History of God
Beyond the Source – Book 1

For more information about any of the above titles, soon to be released titles,
or other items in our catalog, write or visit our website:
PO Box 754, Huntsville, AR 72740
www.ozarkmt.com

Other Books By Ozark Mountain Publishing, Inc.